Contested Representations

Contested Representations

Revisiting
Into the Heart of Africa

Shelley Ruth Butler

Gordon and Breach Publishers

Australia   Canada   China   France   Germany   India
Japan   Luxembourg   Malaysia   The Netherlands
Russia   Singapore   Switzerland

Amsteldijk 166
1st Floor
1079 LH Amsterdam
The Netherlands

Front cover: Single panel from color plate 3, Revised *Into the Heart of Africa* brochure. Courtesy of the Royal Ontario Museum.

Figures 2.1–2.7 and color plates 1–4 are reprinted with permission of the Royal Ontario Museum. Figure 4.1 appears through the courtesy of photographer David Maltby.

Afua Cooper's poem, "The Power of Racism," is reprinted in chapter III with permission of Sister Vision Press, Toronto, Ontario, Canada. Copyright © 1992 Sister Vision Press, Toronto, Ontario, Canada.

The appendix is reprinted with permission of the Coalition for the Truth about Africa.

British Library Cataloguing in Publication Data

Butler, Shelley Ruth
    Contested representations : revisiting "Into the heart of Africa"
    1. Royal Ontario Museum – Exhibitions 2. Museum exhibits – Ontario – Public opinion 3. Ethnology – Africa – Exhibitions 4. Africa – Civilization – Exhibitions
    I. Title
    069.5'09713541

ISBN   90-5700-522-0

For *Norm*

and

In memory of *Geoff*

CONTENTS

ILLUSTRATIONS

Figures

2.1 "For Crown and Empire," installation from *Into the Heart of Africa*.
Photo courtesy of the Royal Ontario Museum.

2.2 "Lord Beresford's Encounter with a Zulu." *Illustrated London News* (1879), featured in "The Imperial Connection" installation from *Into the Heart of Africa*.
Courtesy of the Royal Ontario Museum.

2.3 "Missionary Room" installation from *Into the Heart of Africa*.
Photo courtesy of the Royal Ontario Museum.

2.4 "Ovimbundu Compound" installation from *Into the Heart of Africa*.
Photo courtesy of the Royal Ontario Museum.

2.5 "Africa Room" installation from *Into the Heart of Africa*.
Photo courtesy of the Royal Ontario Museum.

2.6 Advertisement for *Into the Heart of Africa*.
Courtesy of the Royal Ontario Museum.

2.7 Gift Shop at the end of *Into the Heart of Africa*.
Photo courtesy of the Royal Ontario Museum.

4.1 Protestors outside the Royal Ontario Museum.
Photo by David Maltby.

Plates

1 Asante gold necklace in the introductory room of *Into the Heart of Africa*.
Photo courtesy of the Royal Ontario Museum.

2 Original *Into the Heart of Africa* brochure.
Courtesy of the Royal Ontario Museum.

3 Revised *Into the Heart of Africa* brochure.
Courtesy of the Royal Ontario Museum.

4 Promotional image for *Into the Heart of Africa*.
Courtesy of the Royal Ontario Museum.

ACKNOWLEDGMENTS

This book began as a master's thesis in the Dept. of Anthropology at York University in Toronto, Canada. Studying the controversy surrounding *Into the Heart of Africa* at the Royal Ontario Museum was a privilege; it allowed me to move among, and talk to, diverse communities. I felt this when I completed my thesis, and I am even more certain of the value of engaging with difference and relational histories as I write this from Cape Town.

I am grateful to Ken Little at York University for his resourcefulness and ability to be a spirited and engaged advisor. Margaret Rodman, also at York University, provided timely comments that helped me to clarify my arguments. Careful readings of my work were also provided by Beverley Diamond, Ted Magder and Judy Hellman. In a more ephemeral way, my work is indebted to Elvi Whittaker and Claude Bouygues, both of whom communicated a passion for critical and reflexive thought to an impressionable undergraduate at the University of British Columbia. For steadfast friendship that made writing less lonely, I thank Gina Castillo, Catherine Fenn, Cathy Hill, Mona Perusse and Wanda Taylor.

I also benefited from presenting my research at Canadian Anthropology Society (CASCA) meetings, as well as to York undergraduate classes on culture as performance and discourses of colonialism, taught by Ken Little and Teresa Holmes. Financial support for the research was provided by an Ontario Graduate Scholarship as well as by York University.

Julia Matthews and Trilby Bittle gave important assistance at the Royal Ontario Museum, both in the early and final phases of this project. My editor Monica Glina lent fine support and guidance; it was a pleasure to work with her. Finally, thank you to Norman Ravvin, whose readings improve my work and whose care and love sustain it.

Chapter I

Entering the Debates

Introduction: Reading the Royal Ontario Museum

In his widely quoted paper, "The Museum: A Temple or the Forum" (1971), Duncan Cameron distinguishes between two opposing museum stances. The idea of the museum as temple has its origins in the historical moment when private collections in Europe such as royal treasures and cabinets of curiosities—all of which testified to Europe's imperial conquests—were transferred to public hands. Until this development, which occurred a little over a century ago, collections were generally viewed as private, idiosyncratic affairs. If a scholar, for example, had a rare opportunity to view a private collection, the collection was understood to be a reflection of its collector; it spoke of the collector as a world traveler, as a wealthy person, as an eccentric, and so on. But once museums became public, collections took on a new significance. The public, or more accurately, the cultural elite, gained a sense of ownership over museum collections and began to demand that the objects be meaningful to them. In this atmosphere, museums evolved to reflect the values of the establishment that defined (and continues to define) them. For the educated classes, the museum became a temple dedicated to enshrining objects deemed significant and authentic. In short, the museum "represented a standard of excellence. If the museum said that this and that was so, then it was a statement of truth" (Cameron 1971: 17). In this context, the museum visitor experiences the museum as a site of stability. The museum as temple represents

1

(in principle) shared values that the museum visitor is expected to find meaningful and edifying. At such a museum, the individual's

> personal experience of life can be viewed in the context of "The Works of God Through All the Ages; the Arts of Man Through All the Years"
>
> (Cameron 1971: 21)

Thus reads the inscription carved onto the monumental entrance of the Royal Ontario Museum (known as the ROM) in downtown Toronto. However, if the ROM is a quintessential Canadian example of the museum as temple, it has not, in recent years, been completely untouched by the forum. As forum, the museum becomes a site of "confrontation and experimentation" (Cameron 1971: 20), an apt phrase to describe the ROM during its major *Into the Heart of Africa* exhibit.

Into the Heart of Africa showed at the ROM from November 1989 until August 1990, during which time it became the most controversial exhibit in the ROM's history. A measure of the level of controversy is indicated by the fact that when the exhibit closed, four major museums—the Canadian Museum of Civilization, the Vancouver Museum, the Los Angeles County Museum of Natural History, and the Albuquerque Museum of Natural History—canceled their plans to receive it. In Canada, the only precedent for such controversy was the boycott of *The Spirit Sings: Artistic Traditions of Canada's First Peoples,* a major exhibit that showed at the Glenbow Museum in Calgary, Alberta during the 1988 Winter Olympics. By most accounts, *The Spirit Sings* was a respectful and moving exhibit on native heritage and continuity in Canada (Harrison 1988). The boycott, which gained both national and international support, focused on the fact that the exhibit's chief sponsor, Shell Oil, was drilling on land claimed by the Lubicon Lake Cree in northern Alberta. By highlighting the inappropriate and hypocritical nature of this corporate sponsorship, protestors raised awareness about unresolved land claims and the exploitation and marginalization of native peoples in Canada (Trigger 1988). In contrast, the controversy surrounding *Into the Heart of Africa* was deeply enmeshed with the exhibit itself, and with the very question of how we exhibit culture.

Curated by cultural anthropologist Jeanne Cannizzo, *Into the Heart of Africa* attempted to display the ROM's African collection in a critical and reflexive fashion. Drawing on critical strategies associated with postmodernism, Cannizzo attempted to demystify the ROM's aura of ethnographic authority, and to highlight the contingencies and political implications of its practices. Rather than presenting objects from the museum's collection as if they told a story about Africa, Cannizzo challenged her audience to consider their life histories and multiple meanings. This was a fragmentary collection of objects, made up of bequests from families of Canadian missionaries to Africa, as well as from Canadians who served in the army of the British Empire. Approaching the collection as a cultural text, Cannizzo intended to reveal the imperialist ideology of many Canadians at the turn of the century, and in a larger sense, to critique the project of colonial collecting. To this end, Cannizzo re-presented the voices of soldiers and missionaries in an ironic fashion, using quotation marks to highlight their suspect discourses. Phrases such as "the unknown continent," "savage little wars," and "barbarous customs" appeared periodically in quotation marks. However, despite Cannizzo's reflexive focus, *Into the Heart of Africa* was at least partially promoted as a celebration of Africa's cultural and artistic traditions. It is also important to note that this was the ROM's first Africa exhibit, as well as Cannizzo's first opportunity to work as a curator.[1]

Into the Heart of Africa was provocative and generated many divergent readings. Responses to the exhibit can not be characterized as a debate between two monolithic sides—it was not entirely a debate between blacks and whites, nor between the left and the right. In many cases, visitors' various readings of *Into the Heart of Africa* hinged on their response to the exhibit's use of irony and its reflexive stance. Some viewers, for example, appreciated the exhibit's focus on museums and collecting, but felt that its ironic tone was problematic. As anthropologist Jim Freedman wrote:

> The exhibit displays the bounty taken by [conquerors'] hands, bloody hands, without comment or judgement. Unwittingly perhaps, but unquestionably, the exhibit nurtures the swollen pride of those who would see the defeat of the Africans as rightful and the white man's burden as righteous. (1989: 42)

Here, the fact that the exhibit did not make any strong, explicit statement regarding the political and psychological costs of colonialism is seen as dangerously ambiguous. Other visitors, such as the woman who thanked the ROM for a lovely show on "primitive Africa" (in Crean 1991: 26), simply did not get the irony, or Cannizzo's point.

In contrast, some visitors found the exhibit to be a challenging and critical account of museum collecting and imperial ideology. Expressing his appreciation of *Into the Heart of Africa*, journalist Christopher Hume explained: "More than any show I can recall, this one dealt openly and honestly with the 'cultural arrogance'—these are the words used in the display—of our well-intentioned but misguided ancestors" (1990). This reading of the exhibit was, however, deeply challenged by those who claimed that *Into the Heart of Africa* was racist and glorified colonialism. An ad hoc coalition called the "Coalition for the Truth about Africa" (CFTA) renamed the ROM the "Racist Ontario Museum" and held Saturday afternoon protests outside the ROM's entrance. For these protestors, Cannizzo's strategies of representation were not successful. One protestor, for example, explained her reading of the exhibit in the following way:

> I didn't feel good about the show. It was like I was slapped in the face, that was how it felt. [Cannizzo] was trying to depict the activities of the Canadian missionaries and soldiers in Africa, but I don't think, in this day and age, and in this racist country, that that irony was justified.

The exhibit's use of quotation marks around words such as "primitive" was deeply disturbing to these protestors, rendering the ROM, and Cannizzo, suspect. The day after *Into the Heart of Africa* closed, protestors spray-painted Cannizzo's house: "J. Cannizzo is a racist" and "We will never forget J. Cannizzo. We will smash racist colonialism by any means necessary" (quoting Malcolm X).[2] This harassment continued for Cannizzo when she was hired to teach an anthropology course on Africa at the University of Toronto beginning September 1990. Cannizzo eventually resigned from her teaching position, and the debates that had begun at the ROM thoroughly penetrated the academy.

Ironically, on the other side of the political spectrum, missionaries, their families, and academics studying missionaries were also offended by the exhibit. Anthropologist William Samarin, writing in *Christian Week*, presented the following indictment of *Into the Heart of Africa*:

> The exhibit, poorly documented from missionary publications and archives, is specious for its stereotypical view of Christian missions, and it is guilty of making wrong interpretations, blatant contradictions, and frequent speculations in support of its propaganda. (1990: 14)

Finally, one could say that everything that could go wrong, did go wrong with *Into the Heart of Africa*. Such varied and uneven responses to the exhibit clearly undermined the ROM's traditional status as temple and truthteller. Evocative of this crisis is the comment by a black protestor who said to the ROM: "All my life I've been looking for my roots. I come here and you show me nothing."[3] This response contrasts sharply with Cameron's depiction of the museum as a site of stability and personal affirmation.

Coming into the Field

It was in this atmosphere of intense debate that I saw *Into the Heart of Africa* at the ROM during the Summer of 1990. Although I was not working as an anthropologist at the time, I was intrigued by the controversy and the issues it raised concerning the politics of representation. Given my plans to continue my studies in anthropology, and my interest in Africa, I felt quite challenged by the debates.

The controversy raised questions concerning the politics of representation that I had encountered while teaching English in Botswana with Canadian Crossroads International.[4] Although I very much enjoyed living in Botswana, I questioned the post-colonial dynamics of my Crossroads placement. Unequal power relations were reflected, for example, in the English curriculum I taught, which privileged English classics over those of African authors. The critical issue here was one of identity: would students in Botswana reading Robert Louis Stevenson's *Treasure Island* recognize their own experience and history? If not, the risk was that the students would experience the sense of invisibility described by Adrienne Rich: "When someone with the authority of a teacher, say, describes the world and you are not in it, there is a moment of psychic disequilibrium, as if you looked into a mirror and saw nothing" (in Rosaldo 1989: ix). I left Botswana wondering if the extent to which the school curriculum was entwined with the British school system would someday be challenged.

These concerns regarding the decolonization of education were prescient of the ROM controversy. Protestors of *Into the Heart of Africa* contested the ROM's right to ownership of its African collection, as well as the museum's ability to present an exhibit of Africa. The pressure exerted on the ROM is not unfamiliar to curators and anthropologists working in post-colonial societies. George Stocking describes a global trend emerging in the 1960s in which "non-European 'others' whose objects have traditionally filled exhibit halls and cases ... have come forward as actors in the world of museum anthropology" (1985: 10). These encounters have created a space within which museum epistemologies, policies, and practices are being remade. Many mainstream museums now practice some form of consultation and training with minority constituencies, and are involved with repatriation projects (largely in relation to indigenous peoples).[5] However, as the *Into the Heart of Africa* controversy shows, processes of decolonizing museums are far from simple, and are not without contradictions, ambiguities, and points of resistance.

While *Into the Heart of Africa* has an obvious relevance and immediacy in Canada, it has also become (along with *The Spirit Sings*) a touchstone for discussions about the politicization of museums globally.[6] This contradicts a common self-depreciating stereotype that Canada is a "boring" place where nothing important happens. Throughout this book, I will refer to related exhibits from other countries including the United States, England, South Africa, and Zimbabwe. The fact that *Into the Heart of Africa* can help us think about a variety of exhibits produced all over the world reflects two points. First, *Into the Heart of Africa* raises questions about legacies of empire and the representation of black identities, history, and culture that extend beyond national borders. And second, theories and practices of exhibiting culture have local inflections, but also circulate globally.[7]

In the case of *Into the Heart of Africa*, challenges to curatorial authority and institutional power were constructed in a highly personal manner. Protestors questioned the authority and ability of Cannizzo—a white cultural anthropologist—to represent Africa. Thus, lawyer Charles Roach, a prominent member of the CFTA stated: "When the culture of Africans has to be explored and exposed, we have to get African anthropologists involved. Canadian anthropologists can never hope to give justice to the African soul and spirit" (1990: 17). A curious tension developed, as Cannizzo was interested in critically examining how Western museums exhibit Africa, while the CFTA called for an authoritative exhibit that would show "the truth" about Africa. Expressing his disappointment with the exhibit, Ras Rico, a founder of the CFTA, told me that "Cannizzo did not even get close to the heart of Africa."

It was at Victoria Falls in Zimbabwe that I first encountered a representation of the "heart of Africa." A brochure for a safari promised tourists an exciting adventure to the ruins of Bambuzi where the tourist would be able to "feel the presence of a tribe long gone." Later, at Chundu camp, the photographer would be able to "capture the heart of Africa." This safari brochure is a good example of the profound objectification of indigenous peoples that appears in tourist discourse (Little 1991). On safari, indigenous peoples are represented as mythic objects, relics of the past. This objectification is further entrenched at the Victoria Falls Hotel, where blacks silently perform menial duties. It is an atmosphere remarkably devoid of vitality and dialogue.

This problem of objectification played an important role in the controversy at the ROM. Many blacks who objected to *Into the Heart of Africa* explained their feelings in terms of their lack of opportunity to tell their own stories in a major cultural institution such as the ROM. On a pragmatic level, protestors questioned why members of the black community were only minimally consulted during the exhibit's development. And on a more epistemological level, protestors questioned why the exhibit re-presented the voices of Canadian soldiers and missionaries, as opposed to those of Africans. The risk of such a focus is that whiteness becomes a privileged master-text (LaCapra 1991).

It would be dishonest to pretend that I was not both challenged and disturbed by the conflicts that occurred at the ROM. My feelings of ambivalence became most apparent in the context of conducting interviews, when I was often asked to present myself and my views on the exhibit. I would describe my multiple perspectives, never seeming to be able to find one stable position. With regard to the CFTA, for example, I felt sympathetic toward many of the protestors' concerns, as well as a sense of regret over the fact that they could not find an ally in a cultural anthropologist such as Cannizzo.

At the same time, I felt disconcerted by many aspects of the CFTA's discourse, particularly when it pushed towards essentialism. I was very much the "confused critic" described by Kenneth Little (1995) who ponders the intent of a minority group's discourse that seems to replicate dominant ideology.

A similar spirit of ambiguity characterized my positioning with regard to Cannizzo. I felt a sense of identification with her, in her position as a female academic who did her fieldwork in Sierra Leone, who seemed to care about communicating anthropological knowledge to the public, and who was inquisitive about colonial history and ideology. On the other hand, as I became immersed in fieldwork, I felt increasingly critical of particular aspects of her exhibit.

My sense of ambiguous and shifting perspectives with regard to the ROM controversy is well described by Dorinne Kondo who, in her ethnography *Crafting Selves*, suggests that "conflicts, ambiguities, and multiplicities in interpretation, are not simply associated with different positionings in society ... but exist within a 'single' self" (1990: 45). Questioning the Western notion of a single, bounded self, Kondo suggests that we define our selves, and are defined by others, in terms of multiple discourses and shifting subject-positions. This theoretical point became very tangible for me when, during interviews, I shifted between speaking as an anthropologist, a female academic, a community worker, a past Crossroader, and as Jewish.

At times, these self-presentations were strategic on my part. For instance, given the nature of the issues raised by the ROM controversy, it is perhaps not surprising that I often felt conscious of being "another white anthropologist" during my fieldwork. One way that I dealt with this discomfort was by presenting myself as Jewish, a shorthand way of saying "white but not white." This was a way of signaling that I too feel threatened by a spray-painted wall that reads "White Power," and that I am not completely at home in the white establishment.[8] In particular, in a few interviews, I drew upon my experience as the daughter of a survivor of Terezin to create a space for discussing the challenges of living with traumatic histories and images. This identification became important since many critiques of *Into the Heart of Africa* depended upon making an analogy with representations of the Holocaust. The Holocaust served as a reference point for protestors who felt that their own subjugation was being misrepresented by the ROM.

Though I feel challenged by the complexity of my multiple relationships to the ROM controversy, I also appreciate how this level of difficulty helps to create new understanding and meaning. In this sense, my anthropology is personal and subjective and does not pretend to be otherwise. This sense of my own multiplicity has become a model for respecting and exploring the complex ways in which people position themselves and construct identity in relation to the controversy, the exhibit, Cannizzo, and the CFTA.

Museum Ethnography

The ROM is located in downtown Toronto, close to the University of Toronto. This is also the neighborhood that I lived in, making the expression "anthropology at home" very apropos. The first step in my research on *Into the Heart of Africa* was to request the text of the exhibit as well as press clippings from the ROM. What I received proved to be very revealing in terms of what was, and was not, included in this package. Most significantly, an internal report (Crawford, Hankel and Rowse 1990) on the controversy that was originally prepared for the public, but later redirected to the board of directors, was not included. (I received this report from a past employee of the ROM and it was also leaked to other members of the public.) Other documents that individuals gave to me also reflected particular ways of framing the controversy.

After collecting documentation, I conducted interviews with a variety of people involved in, or touched by, the controversy. These included museum professionals, academics, curators, members of the black community, members of the CFTA, and students in the fields of anthropology, museum studies, history, and film. In choosing who to interview, my goal was to bring together and juxtapose different perspectives on the ROM controversy, and to examine the intersections of these voices. In this sense my ethnography is driven by themes, images, and issues, as opposed to a more traditional focus on a particular community or geographic area.

I made complete transcripts of the interviews, offering them to each person I interviewed. This was a way of creating a measure of personal accountability since I made it clear to the person I was interviewing that they were welcome to make changes or corrections to the transcript if certain phrases appeared incorrect, or somehow out of context. Many people I interviewed seemed to feel relieved by this opportunity, having had frustrating experiences talking with journalists. This realization marked the beginning of my interest in the question of media coverage of the controversy. I am especially concerned with the media's suppression of ambiguity, a topic I will return to during my discussion of constructions of the controversy.

I also transcribed interviews so that I could become immersed, if only briefly, in the idioms of the people I interviewed. In considering responses to the ROM controversy, I want to pay close attention to people's speech and experiences, as opposed to mapping out static, discrete, positions in the debate. This strategy can be situated in the theoretical context of critiques of structuralism that challenge anthropologists to pay attention to individual speech and the creative production of language. By recognizing the structuralist legacy of considering language to be a monolithic, static system, we can begin to understand language as a field of contention and conflict. In the context of the ROM controversy, we can also appreciate language as performative. Language, as Terry Eagleton explains, "achieves something *in the saying*" (1983: 118). In this light, language is social action, a point that I will return to during my discussion of the CFTA.

I decided not to interview Jeanne Cannizzo for a number of reasons. On a pragmatic level, she no longer lived in Canada. But more importantly, I felt that the controversy had become too personalized and this is one interpretation that I want to challenge. My decision was also influenced by the fact that Cannizzo wrote a detailed post-mortem on *Into the Heart of Africa* and its controversy, which was published in *Visual Anthropology Review* (1991). I draw on this piece, as well as other statements Cannizzo made in the *Toronto Star* (1990a) and in response to Enid Shildkrout's review of *Into the Heart of Africa* in *Museum Anthropology* (1991b). In each of these pieces, Cannizzo never expresses regret over any aspect of her exhibit, or the way in which it was developed.

Translating my fieldwork experience into writing posed particular dilemmas. First, some people whom I interviewed wanted their privacy to be protected. Ironically, some of these peoples' names have already appeared in the public record, yet it was still important to them to have a guarantee of confidentiality. This is a good indicator of the level of emotional intensity that many people experienced throughout the controversy. One student protestor, for example, prefaced his request for anonymity with a description of an uncomfortable experience where a professor in his department aggressively attempted to make a case defending Cannizzo and the exhibit. As he explained, he wanted his privacy to be protected because he did not want "further repercussions." Another graduate student who requested that her identity be protected, recounted her experience of feeling "boxed in" and unsure of how to respond to the controversy. As a student of African art and history, she described how she felt a sense of professional responsibility to address what she called the "historical inaccuracies" of the exhibit. On the other hand, she was reluctant to speak out, for she did not want to "gang up on a victim" (meaning Cannizzo). Above all, this person was conscious of her own vulnerability as a Ph.D. student who would soon be on the job market. To respect these people's right to privacy, I will occasionally refer abstractly to "one protestor" or to "one curator," and so on.

A second challenge regarding the process of translating my fieldwork experience into writing is related to the difficulty of knowing where my voice ends, and where those of others I have interviewed begin. This dilemma reflects the productive nature of fieldwork. Many of my ideas about *Into the Heart of Africa* evolved in the course of interviews, where people offered their own analysis of the exhibit and the issues which they felt it raised. In writing about *Into the Heart of Africa*, I want to acknowledge the variety of opinions and ideas held by people touched by the controversy, as well as to develop my own analysis of the issues. In this way, my writing deals with the same issues of voice and authority that permeate the ROM controversy. Above all, I do not want my own voice to dominate those of other participants in these debates.

Writing about *Into the Heart of Africa* also poses another kind of predicament; like Cannizzo (and most other critics writing about *Into the Heart of Africa*), I use quotation marks in a number of different ways and am counting on readers to be able to decode them.[9] First, I use quotation marks around expressions like "the unknown continent" and "civilized," in order to signal their problematic or highly charged nature. Here I practice a form of cultural criticism that seeks to examine how such terms are constituted and deployed. In a similar vein, I use quotation marks to highlight terms that I am exploring in a critical fashion, such as the idea that there exists an "exact" or "true" representation of reality. That my use of quotation marks is similar to the practice of using them to signal irony is not surprising since critical inquiry often demands that attention be paid to the ironies and ambiguities of cultural forms and practices. Finally, I also use quotation marks to cite other authors' work and to quote people whom I interviewed, as is standard academic practice.

Looking Ahead

The *Into the Heart of Africa* controversy provides us with rich and important material. It is not surprising that the exhibit and its resulting controversy have been described as crystallizing "the accomplishments and challenges facing museums and museologists in the next decade" (Baeker, May and Tivy 1992: 123). On the one hand, the exhibit teaches us about the possibilities and pitfalls of reflexive curatorship. And, in a larger sense, the exhibit's controversy allows us to do an anthropology of public culture (Ames 1992, Karp 1992) and to consider current social, political, and intellectual forces affecting museums and minority constituencies.

Many people I interviewed referred to problems in the exhibit by saying something like, "It was a case of good intentions gone astray" (some protestors, however, would find this comment too generous). In any case, this comment is interesting because it reveals an irony that shapes much of the controversy. Cannizzo made many explicit statements in which she expressed her commitment to dispelling negative stereotypes of Africa, to confronting colonialism, and to fighting racism (Cannizzo 1990a, 1991a).[10] Ironically, many protestors would agree with these goals, and do articulate similar concerns. So we have to ask, what went wrong? Why was productive dialogue between protestors and Cannizzo, and between protestors and the ROM, so impossible? While I do not think that there is any single answer to these questions, this study of *Into the Heart of Africa* offers a variety of suggestions

regarding what went wrong. Some points are related to poor curatorial decisions, some to the structural problem of presenting a critical exhibit from
within an establishment museum such as the ROM, and some relate to the
larger social and political context of Toronto in the 1990s. As Martin Klein,
a professor of African history said: "What I'm now conscious of, partly as
a result of the ROM [controversy], is that we're going to have a problem here
in Toronto."

My starting point for this study of *Into the Heart of Africa* is to examine
Cannizzo's curatorial strategies and goals in order to situate her work in
a larger intellectual and museological context. This discussion begins in
Chapter Two, where I also present a close reading of *Into the Heart of Africa*,
paying particular attention to its political and semiotic ambiguity. This ambiguity forms an important context for examining the complexity of responses to
the exhibit.

In Chapter Three I consider the prelude to the controversy; the early
positive reviews of the exhibit, as well as the first contestations over the
exhibit brochure. Responses to the exhibit brochure raise a number of important issues related to public expectations of museums, public resistance to
reflexive museology, and the politics of exhibiting culture in multicultural
and post-colonial contexts.

Chapter Four traces the escalation of the controversy and examines constructions of it, by drawing on my fieldwork and a wide variety of documents. These include: an internal report from the ROM, newspaper and
magazine articles, a Toronto Board of Education report, minutes from Town
Hall Meetings (organized by and for the black community), poetry and a
video created by black artists, and articles and memos written by academics.
In this way, I do not treat museums as bounded sites. Rather, the controversy
at the ROM demonstrates the way in which museums are just one site
amongst a broader topography where struggles over re-presenting history
occur (Simon 1994). While museums such as the Royal Ontario Museum are
associated with such qualities as permanence and legitimacy, other exhibitionary sites and strategies—such as the pamphlets produced by the CFTA—
are more informal, ephemeral, and performative (Kirshenblatt-Gimblett
1990, de Certeau 1988).

In Chapter Five I focus on the discourse of the CFTA. The fact that the
CFTA confidently contested the ROM's depiction of Africa can be situated in
the context of postmodernism, which challenges "authoritative visions of
what constitutes History" (Hutcheon 1991: 140). This theoretical impulse
appears to have thoroughly penetrated life beyond the academy, at least in
multicultural cities such as Toronto. Witness, for example, the enormous
interest in history, and in reclaiming and remaking history, that 1992
Quincentenary "commemorations" of Columbus generated.[11] But the ideological atmosphere of the CFTA is not without ambiguity. While the CFTA

discourse challenges the idea of the ROM as truth-teller, the CFTA claim to know "the truth" about Africa. This claim seems distant from postmodernism's suspicion of the "very idea of truth" (Hawthorn in Spivak 1990: 18). More importantly, this use of the term "truth" marks just one of many moments of creative tension in the CFTA discourse. In considering such tensions within the CFTA discourse, I emphasize the ambiguous, contradictory, and at times strategic nature of resistance.

I also consider the CFTA from the point of view of the anthropology of performance, examining how the coalition used their demonstrations to address a wide variety of issues concerning racism and representation in Canadian society. These issues included police racism, educational racism, affirmative action at the ROM, and the elitist structure of the ROM board of directors. In this sense, protestors became an integral part of the exhibit text, extending it beyond the walls of the museum to touch current concerns in the black community (Philip 1991). Significantly, many people who did not fully agree with the strategies or rhetoric of the CFTA, still credit them with raising awareness about issues of concern to members of the black community. As Tara Chadwick, an anthropology student who worked at the ROM during the controversy, said with regard to the impact of the CFTA: "I think that people in Toronto are going to be a lot more aware and a lot more sensitive to Eurocentrism."

Chapter Five examines responses to, and constructions of, the CFTA. In particular, I highlight the complexity of the controversy by noting how people struggled to define themselves in relation to the CFTA (and by extension, to the ROM and Cannizzo). Finally, my concluding remarks refer to broader questions about the way in which *Into the Heart of Africa* has been canonized, and to its lasting local and transnational significance to debates about theory and practice in museums.

Final Notes on the Forum

A museum, according to Duncan Cameron, must choose between the distinct positions of temple and forum. It cannot be both. As Cameron writes, the forum's "admittance to the museum (even a swinging museum) is acceptance by the Establishment" (1971: 20). Or, as Barbara Kirshenblatt-Gimblett succinctly puts it, "carnival represented is carnival tamed" (1991: 433). But I hesitate to suggest that the forum has completely disappeared from the ROM, now that *Into the Heart of Africa* has closed and the Saturday afternoon protests and confrontations with the police dim in the public memory. To borrow Kirshenblatt-Gimblett's phrase, I am not sure if carnival represented is, necessarily, carnival tamed. Consider, for example, *Caribbean Celebrations*, an exhibit that showed at the ROM from June until September 1991, less than a year after the closing of *Into the Heart of Africa*. This exhibit of Caribbean carnival costumes was chiefly developed by the Saint Louis Art Museum. However, the ROM employed local curator Hazel Da Breo to create a special display of costumes from Toronto Caribbana festivals. One costume that Da Breo exhibited was called "The Princess of the Saryangetty" and was part of the 1990 Caribbana festival, which was held soon after the *Into the Heart of Africa* controversy. An exhibit panel situated the stunning costume in a broader historical and semiotic context:

> In Caribbana 1990, the masquerade band "Beyond the Darkness" attempted to counter the negative stereotype of Africa as "the dark continent" by celebrating the creative energy that infuses African culture.

Clearly, "The Princess of the Saryangetty" is intended to be an oppositional artistic production, one which challenges dominant stereotypes of Africa. But what happens when this costume is displayed within an elitist museum such as the ROM? Is it still oppositional, or is it now tamed? I doubt that there is a simple answer to this question. However, it is interesting to imagine "The Princess of the Saryangetty" as a response to issues raised by *Into the Heart of Africa*. A major concern for protestors of *Into the Heart of Africa* was their sense that the exhibit reiterated (despite Cannizzo's critical intentions) negative stereotypes of Africa. In contrast, the exhibit text accompanying "The Princess of the Saryangetty" makes its critical intentions clear. In this way, "The Princess of the Saryangetty" succeeded (for this visitor) in bringing protestors' concerns about representation inside the ROM. The temple is not quite what it was, and it is precisely this sense of the ongoing life of issues raised by the *Into the Heart of Africa* controversy—as opposed to closure—that I want to evoke in the following pages.

Chapter II

Into the Heart of Africa and the Status Quo

The Status Quo

Tourists, including those visiting a museum, want "the real thing." As tourists, we typically search for all that is authentic, pristine, and genuine.[1] Natural history and anthropology museums respond to this nostalgia for the authentic by offering visitors exhibits of exotic others, other worlds, worlds long past. This is why Richard Handler calls our museums modern "temples of authenticity" (1986: 4). At the museum, tourists view objects that metonymically stand for the culture of their creators. By viewing these ethnographic fragments, visitors can experience and appropriate authenticity. Moreover, no twentieth-century museum is without a souvenir shop, which allows visitors to purchase a possession—a specimen or trophy of the exotic—of their own. My own experience of feeling lured into souvenir shops before having even visited the exhibits suggests the extent to which shopping has become an important part of the museum experience.[2]

In *On Longing: Narratives of the Miniature, the Gigantic, the Souvenir, the Collection* (1984), Susan Stewart describes the appeal of these souvenirs. Souvenirs of the exotic promise Western consumers access to a "primitive" world, which is popularly associated with simplicity and innocence, and exists as a (mythic) alternative to the complexities of modernity. By owning an exotic souvenir, we appropriate its foreignness. The ethnographic fragment becomes a part of the possessor's story. As museum tourists we say, "I bought this mask during my visit to *Into the Heart of Africa*." To own a souvenir is thus to move "history into private time" (Stewart 1984: 138).

This desire to rescue authenticity is not limited to tourists, for it plays a significant role in the history of anthropology. Early twentieth-century anthropologists worked with a sense of urgency to record and collect the cultures of non-Western peoples whom they believed would soon disappear completely in the face of Western expansion and imperialism. This salvage mission dominated early twentieth-century anthropology, and coincided with the discipline's early efforts to establish itself as a science of man dedicated to charting human development and progress. Anthropologists collected and preserved tribal objects deemed endangered, classifying the objects as cultural artifacts or, as was done later in the twentieth century, as aesthetic works of art.[3] The result of these processes of classification is that the active history of non-Western peoples is suppressed. Non-Western cultures become a footnote to Western history. As James Clifford writes, "we produce authenticity by removing objects from their current historical situation" (1988: 228). The political stakes of salvage anthropology are particularly apparent in the context of museum representations. In *The Tourist* (1976), Dean MacCannel describes museums as playing a critical role in reinforcing the ideological separation of the West from the non-West. MacCannel writes: "The best indication of the final victory of modernity is not the disappearance of the non-modern world, but its artificial presentation and reconstruction in modern society" (1976: 8). Thus, although museum professionals often argue that museums can play a role in diminishing ethnocentrism and racial tensions, MacCannel's less optimistic perspective emphasizes the unequal power relations inherent in the practice of collecting and exhibiting the world.[4] This is a perspective that culture critics such as James Clifford (1988) and Marianna Torgovnick (1990), as well as curators such as Michael Ames (1992), Christina Kreps (1988), Susan Vogel (1989), and Jane Peirson Jones (1992) are currently addressing. Jeanne Cannizzo certainly fits into this group of scholars and curators. It is telling, for example, that both Michael Ames (1986: 32) and Christiana Kreps (1988: 56) cite Cannizzo's work on museums as representative of the future direction of reflexive and critical curating.

Towards a Reflexive Museology

Whereas curators have traditionally focused on the goals of acquiring and preserving objects, and have been preoccupied with presenting artifacts in reconstructions of their "original settings," reflexive museology changes the way in which we think about museums and their collections. Focusing on museum practices of collecting, classifying, and displaying material culture, reflexive museology is informed by the premise that exhibits of other cultures are neither neutral nor tropeless, despite claims otherwise. Rather, exhibits are informed by the cultural, historical, institutional, and political contexts of the people who make them (Lavine 1989). Seminal statements on reflexive museology call for curators to create exhibits that draw attention to the processes by which museums recontextualize objects (Halpin 1983) and to engage audiences as active interpreters of exhibits (Shelton 1990).[5] Both of these notions have the potential to disrupt traditional museum epistemology in which viewers are assumed to be "selves" who seek in museums displays of "others." Significantly, Anthony Shelton names this critical approach post-modern museology. The term is useful to note since, although Cannizzo never uses the term postmodern in her own writing, many critics view *Into the Heart of Africa* as an example of postmodern cultural criticism. As we shall see, one way in which *Into the Heart of Africa* is now canonized, is as an example in a much larger debate about the politics of postmodernism and public culture.

In developing her critical ideas about museums, Cannizzo draws from theory developed in cultural anthropology and literary criticism. Interpretive anthropologist Clifford Geertz is a central presence in Cannizzo's work, both in her academic research on performance in Sierra Leone (1983) and in her applied work as a culture critic whose voice has been heard on the Canadian Broadcasting Corporation's "Ideas" program (1982, 1987b, 1989b, 1991b). In particular, Cannizzo makes use of the culture as text metaphor which Geertz popularized in anthropology. Considering museum exhibits as texts, Cannizzo interprets their cultural meanings. For instance, in her first involvement with museums over a decade ago, Cannizzo worked for the British Columbia Museums Association making recommendations regarding the training needs of curators in local museums. In conducting this research, Cannizzo developed an analysis of the ideology of the exhibits she found in local museums. She pointed out that these museums have a tendency to present idealized visions of a pastoral and harmonious past, not unlike Robert Redfield's depictions of Tepoztlan. Cannizzo questioned curators as to why issues concerning ethnicity, class, and gender were not addressed in these museums. In response to her queries, curators explained to Cannizzo that they felt that they performed an important public service by reminding museum visitors—who they felt were largely "rootless, modern [and] urban" (Cannizzo 1989b: 156)—of bygone days.

By interpreting the meanings of exhibits, Cannizzo works as a culture critic, demystifying the museum. And unlike many culture critics in the academy, Cannizzo is committed to communicating and demonstrating these critical skills to the general public. Reading Cannizzo's work on museums, I am reminded of Nadya Aisenberg and Mona Harrington's observation that many women who enter the academy and teaching are motivated by a desire to recreate for others their own empowering experience of learning (1988: 39). Thus, while curators traditionally align themselves with science and objectivity, Cannizzo teaches her audience the basic anthropological lesson that even the most natural arrangements are in fact cultural, as well as shaped

by political forces. And while traditional curators focus on the function of
museums (to collect, to preserve), Cannizzo and other young critics focus on
intellectual and ethical issues relating to the purpose of museums (to inform,
to educate, to empower, and so on) (Weil 1990: 51).

Cannizzo seems particularly moved by the idea that museums can
empower their audiences. She writes enthusiastically about the potential
"subversive" effect of telling history, and she imagines exhibits that will
address issues of conflict (1987b: 20). This is a significant challenge, especially considering that museums typically have a very conservative outlook.
This conservative bias can be traced to the museum's focus on preservation,
the general expectation that museums should present celebratory stories, and
finally, their dependence upon government funding (Ames 1992). It is interesting to note that the Vancouver Museum canceled *Into the Heart of Africa*
due to fear of potential community backlash and difficulty in securing corporate sponsorship for the controversial exhibit.[6]

In her earlier writings on museums, Cannizzo presents herself not only
as a culture critic, but also as a populist. She defends, for example, the right
of local museums to present their own exhibits and versions of the past.
Comparing exhibits created by Canada's "curatorial class" (1989: 156) to
those created by local curators, Cannizzo writes:

> The question is not one of truthfulness as I see it. That is, it's not which model
> more fully represents the facts of the matter. What's at issue is the role of
> increasing professionalization in the museum field, a process which runs the risk
> of promoting a standardized vision of history. (1982: 8)

Here, Cannizzo's statement reflects her understanding of knowledge as being
socially constructed, and her sense that historical narratives are selective and
always involve interpretation. Such a theoretical position disturbs the traditional
authority of curators, who have acted as gatekeepers, identifying themselves as
the privileged few who can decode museum collections (Jenkinson 1989).

Cannizzo's apparent populist sensibility coincides very closely with
John Urry's depiction of postmodern museums, where we find a broadening
in the range of objects and histories deemed deserving of being preserved and
represented to the public (1990: 129). In *The Tourist Gaze* (1990), Urry
describes how museum visitors are increasingly intrigued by displays of the
ordinary, such as a representation of the daily life of soldiers in a British garri-
son. Urry sees this proliferation of local histories of the mundane in museums
as reflecting postmodernism's anti-elitist politics. Here, Urry follows critics
who stress postmodernism's valorization of mass culture and its mixing of
codes borrowed from high and low culture (Giroux 1988). However, despite
Cannizzo's interest in democratizing museums, *Into the Heart of Africa* was
often accused of being elitist and exclusionary (Lyons and Lyons n.d., Mackey

1995). This critique, in turn, became a tool for arguing that postmodernism serves the interests of the cultural elite, a point I will return to (and question) in my Afterword.

Cannizzo's interest in democratizing museums is reflected in her original proposal for an African exhibit at the ROM (in Crawford, Hankel and Rowse 1990: 4–5). A major aim for Cannizzo was to broaden the visitor base of the ROM, which is notorious for attracting a well-educated, predominantly white audience. In fact, this clientele dominated the attendance of *Into the Heart of Africa*.[7] It appears that Cannizzo and the ROM took few steps to include and reach a black audience, an issue which, as we shall see, was central to the CFTA's concerns. In any case, it is important to take note of Cannizzo's call for the democratization of museums. Now, by looking closely at *Into the Heart of Africa* in light of Cannizzo's curatorial goals, we can gain a sense of the complexity of creating an oppositional exhibit in an establishment, bureaucratic museum. As well, we can gain insight into the possibilities and the risks of reflexive museology.

Re-presenting Imperialism: A Personal Walk Through the
Exhibit After the Fact

Into the Heart of Africa included some 375 objects collected in Africa between 1870 and 1925. As well, the exhibit included a large number of archival materials, such as photographs of Canadian missionary stations and Canadian military officers in Africa, illustrations from popular accounts of explorers and missionaries in Africa, reproductions of newspaper articles reporting imperial advances, and photographs of Africans taken by Canadians. The exhibit had five distinct areas: the Imperial Connection, the Military Hall, the Missionary Room, the Ovimbundu Compound, and the Africa Room. While the first four phases of the exhibit focused on imperialist ideology, colonial collecting, and the museum's implication in this project, the final room was promoted as a celebration of African cultural and artistic traditions. What follows is a brief tour of *Into the Heart of Africa*, where I highlight images, objects, and texts that I think are either significant to the controversy, or are strong indicators of Cannizzo's museological and intellectual influences.

Entering *Into the Heart of Africa*, the visitor was immediately confronted by re-presentations of imperialist ideology. The introductory panel to the exhibit read:

Africa in the 19th century was still "the unknown continent" to most Canadians. Ignorance promoted powerful images of a mysterious land full of "barbarous" peoples. But Canadian soldiers and missionaries became full participants in the New Imperialism of Queen Victoria's later reign. They ventured through savannah and rainforest, encountering unfamiliar cultures with world views radically different from their own.

This introductory panel set the tone for the first half of the exhibit, where voices and perspectives of Canadian collectors, soldiers, and missionaries were presented. Cannizzo used quotation marks in order to signal the corrupt nature of these discourses; words such as "the unknown continent" and "barbarous" appeared periodically in quotes. This subtle use of irony was risky, especially given that visitors typically understand museums to be authoritative truth-tellers; many visitors did not understand the irony and read phrases such as "savage little wars" or "barbarous customs" literally. To understand the irony of the exhibit's texts, a certain amount of shared knowledge with the curator was required. *Into the Heart of Africa* asked its viewers to perceive its artifacts and language historically, since the words in quotation marks always referred to past practices and ideology. Unfortunately, viewers who did not have a fairly high level of education were not likely to have the academic or cultural capital to grasp these various meanings. To paraphrase Pierre Bourdieu (1984: 2–4), the capacity to see (voir) is always a function of knowledge (savoir).

Others missed the irony as a result of simply not reading the exhibit panels, a practice that is very common to museum-goers.[8] Museums are very much the domain of objects, not texts. These visitors also missed the explicit disclaimers included in the exhibit, such as this statement which appeared in the Missionary Room, at the entrance to a small nook where visitors watched a recreation of a missionary lantern show: "The sense of cultural superiority and paternalism that you will hear in this fictional narrative was characteristic of the missionary world view at the time." On the other hand, many people understood the irony, and recognized the disclaimers, but still found the ironic tone inappropriate, a point that I will return to when I discuss responses to the exhibit.

Good exhibits are often "conceptually simple" (Gurian 1990). It follows that successful exhibits are often those that do not require a high level of literacy, as difficult label copy too often creates a barrier, alienating those who cannot understand. Thus, ambiguous uses of language—as in the choice of the exhibit's title which played on both Conrad's *Heart of Darkness* (1902) and on the legacy of accounts by explorers and missionaries of "dark Africa"—risked alienating many visitors. The exhibit language might easily be interpreted as being "part of the paraphernalia which always announces the sacred character, separate and separating, of high culture—the icy solemnity of the great museum, the grandiose luxury of the opera-houses and major theaters, the decor and decorum of concert-halls" (Bourdieu 1984: 34). In her article "Noodling around with Exhibition Opportunities" (1990), Elaine Heuman Gurian proposes a number of strategies that curators can follow in order to make their exhibits more accessible and more inclusive. Techniques such as defining all terms, providing an introduction to contextualize the exhibit, and locating geographical references are all useful and fairly straight-forward ideas.

However, it is important to appreciate the particular challenge an exhibit such as *Into the Heart of Africa* poses to a curator, as a position must be devised from which to critique the images that are being presented. It is worthwhile to note briefly the strategies of critique used in two other exhibits, *Degenerate Art* and *The Other Museum*, which showed at about the same time as *Into the Heart of Africa*.

Degenerate Art: The Fate of the Avant-Garde in Nazi Germany (Los Angeles County Museum of Art 1991) provides an interesting point of compari-son since, like *Into the Heart of Africa*, it dealt with the issue of re-presenting hurtful and racist ideology. *Degenerate Art* presented Nazi ideology by reconstructing the *Entartete Kunst* exhibition of 1937 (Barron 1991). This was an art exhibition designed by the Third Reich to ridicule contemporary visual art, which the Nazis judged to be morally degenerate. In 1937 the Reich appropriated from German museums some 16,000 paintings, sculp-tures, drawings and prints deemed alternately "art-Bolshevism," "barbarism of representation," or simply "Jewish art." Of these, some 650 pieces were displayed in the *Entartete Kunst* (*Degenerate Art*) exhibit, which opened in Munich and then traveled throughout Germany for four years. The original exhibit was a showpiece for Nazi political, aesthetic, and racial ideology.

The challenge for the contemporary *Degenerate Art* exhibit was to both recreate, and to contextualize the spirit under which the Nazis attacked pre-World War II trends in art. The design of *Degenerate Art* was critical for establishing its moral tone. Especially important were the first rooms, which prepared visitors for what was to follow. Designed by architect Frank Gehry, these rooms created a sense of Germany in the 1930s and the rise of the Third Reich. Visitors saw documentary films of Goebbels' speeches, book burnings, and Nazi parades. Display cases were filled with Nazi propaganda brochures. And in one room, visitors listened to tapes of émigrés describing their stories of fleeing Nazi Germany, as well as to the haunting ballads from Brecht and Weil's *Threepenny Opera*. After this emo-tionally stirring "sensory overload," (Loughery 1992: 524), visitors entered the re-constructed *Entartete Kunst* show. By this time, visitors had a clear sense of what they were witnessing. The violence of Nazism was exposed, and this exposition was transformed into a means for public education.

The Other Museum (1991) was curated by Fred Wilson and showed at the Washington Project for the Arts. As Enid Schildkrout (1991) has pointed out, the exhibit shared a number of themes with *Into the Heart of Africa*, such as collecting, representation, and colonialism. Moreover, like *Into the Heart of Africa*, *The Other Museum* used irony in order to present its critical perspective. As in the case of *Degenerate Art*, visitors were well-prepared for the exhibit: before entering, they were given a black and yellow brochure that parodied *National Geographic*. A statement inside the brochure explained that Wilson's motivation for curating the exhibit was his urge to examine the "colonialist roots of Western ethnography." The brochure further explained that Wilson labeled objects on display with ironic texts, and assembled them to mimic a natural history museum.

Ironic cues in *The Other Museum* were obvious, dramatic, and playful (Schildkrout 1991). The words "other" and "ourselves" were, for example, always displayed upside down. A series of photographs taken by colonialists, which had the same atmosphere of objectification that haunted the photographs in *Into the Heart of Africa*, was entitled "Photographs by Others." This series was contrasted with a series of more sensitive photographs of indigenous peoples entitled, "Photographs by Ourselves." Clearly, *The Other Museum* succeeded in re-presenting the language and visual codes of colonialists in a critical tone.

In making these comments, it is important to note that both *Degenerate Art* and *The Other Museum* are the product of art galleries, not natural history museums. Given the recent art controversies surrounding Robert Mapplethorpe's photographs as well as Jana Sterbak's flesh dress, it seems very likely that art galleries are more easily politicized than natural history and anthropological museums such as the ROM (Wigington 1991). In contrast to art galleries, natural history museums are strongly associated with the pure sciences and the presentation of "objective facts."[9] Given this, visitors to natural history museums also expect visual images and texts to convey a consistent message, a convention that Cannizzo's use of irony ignored (Hutcheon 1994). Finally, in the context of the ROM, it appears that the "primitivist tropes" (Torgovnick 1990) that *Into the Heart of Africa* critically presented—such as the myth of the dark continent—were sometimes taken at face value.

It is useful to situate such readings of the ROM in a larger historical context. To begin to understand why some people felt suspicious of the ROM's intentions, we need to be aware of the legacy of how Europe has interpreted and represented "the primitive." By the nineteenth century, an unequal relationship between Europe and the "dark continent" had long been established. Europe considered Africa to be its extreme opposite, its inverted self-image. The rise of the life sciences, with their preoccupation with the "great chain of being," entrenched Africa's lowly place in the hierarchy of human development.[10]

Significantly, these "findings" were represented in the first public museums. Capitalizing on public interest in racial typologies and evolution, it was not unusual for museums to use realist wax mannequins to create "types of Mankind" and "Great Human Family" exhibits. At one museum, visitors could even compare portraits of great men to those of "savages." Visitors could also take home, as a souvenir, a portrait of their own silhouette, reproduced by the museum's "physignotrace" machine (Kirshenblatt-Gimblett 1991: 398–401). In short, we can say that museums have played a central role in reifying and legitimizing images of "the primitive."

Despite these inheritances, Cannizzo wanted to create a critical, reflexive exhibit at the ROM. Rather than present an authoritative, "authentic" exhibit on African cultures, Cannizzo used the ROM's African collection to examine both Canadian and African sensibilities. As Cannizzo explains, the objects of the ROM collection are an expression "not only of the world view of those who chose to make and use them, but also of those who chose to collect and exhibit them" (1991a: 151). Thus, for Cannizzo, an artifact such as a Yoruba mask has multiple meanings depending upon the context in which we view it: museum visitors can consider the mask, now as ritual object, now as missionary souvenir, now as museum artifact. Cannizzo describes her own process of discovering these narratives: "As I spent hour upon hour in the Museum storeroom... dialogues seemed to emerge from the masks, baskets, sculptures, and beadwork in which they had been embodied for generations" (1989a: 10). I will say more about the politics of this statement later, but for now, I want simply to stress Cannizzo's sense of discovering multiple and shifting narratives in her effort to tell the story of *Into the Heart of Africa*. This "relational approach" (Clifford 1992: 218) allows Cannizzo to study the social history of the ROM's African collection, as well as the role of museums in shaping Western perceptions of Africa. In this way, the ROM's African collection becomes more than just a relic of an exotic past. It symbolizes complex colonial and post-colonial relations.

The introductory room of *Into the Heart of Africa* subtly suggested to visitors the complex, multiple issues that Cannizzo was attempting to address. Graphic panels showing a British military scouting party and missionaries in Africa were meant to suggest the theme of colonial encounters that shaped the exhibit. A few objects, such as a stunning Asante gold necklace, were handsomely displayed to show their beauty (see Plate 1). Cannizzo writes that these objects were displayed in order to "refute the 19th-century Canadian supposition of barbarism" (1991a: 152).

In the following room, called "The Imperial Connection," the visitor was once again immersed in imperial ideology. Displays such as a page of Canadian Reverend Banfield's English Nupe Dictionary and a page from Stanley's *Heroes of the Dark Continent* (1890) were used to suggest that artifacts are symbolic of colonial relations, and to consider the production of nineteenth-century images of "dark Africa." Amidst military memorabilia, visitors saw a display of a Canadian officer's pith helmet, (ironically) displayed on a pedestal in a soft light and a plexiglass box (see Figure 2.1).

Interestingly, the ceiling of the Imperial Connection was partially covered with a large Union Jack flag. Visitors seemed to be literally enveloped

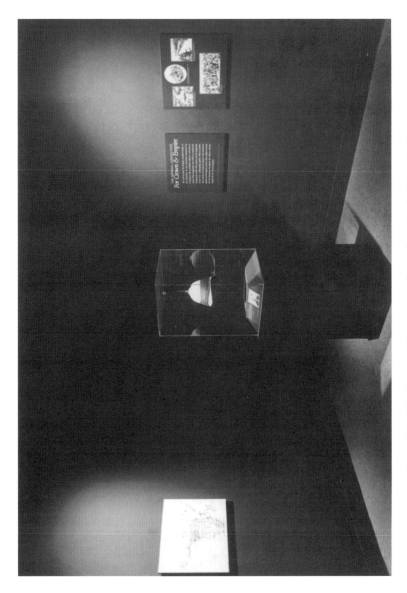

Figure 2.1 "For Crown and Empire," installation from *Into the Heart of Africa.*

in the imperialist ideology. In a post-mortem review of the exhibit, Cannizzo offers a revealing analysis of this presentation. She writes:

> The design for the suite of rooms was to suggest a "Victorian" look and the ceiling was partially covered by a large Union Jack of the design common at the turn of the century, reminding visitors of Canada's own colonial status and establishing the imperial connection yet further. The rich dark blue of this room recalled to me the intensity of the West African sky: to other members of the design team it suggested the Britishness of English-speaking Canada at the time. (1991a: 153)

Here Cannizzo's fond memory of the blue African sky is curiously enmeshed with the image of imperial blue that she is supposedly critiquing. Cannizzo's romantic memories of Africa are entangled with her critical project. This is an example of the complex problems which are posed by re-presenting imperial ideology. In very subtle ways, the academic or curator risks either replicating or internalizing the very ideology being analyzed (LaCapra 1989: 37). As well, because we generally look at flags with a sense of admiration and respect, there was a risk that visitors might miss the critique completely and identify with imperialism's triumphalism.

The most controversial image of the exhibit was found in the next room, the Military Hall. This image was an enlarged engraving depicting Lord Beresford thrusting his sword into a Zulu man. The engraving was reproduced from the *Illustrated London News* of September 1879, along with its original caption, "Lord Beresford's Encounter with a Zulu" (see Figure 2.2). Significantly, this image of European conquest was not directly addressed. Nor was the propagandistic aspect of the engraving made explicit, a problem when we consider that typically the public views newspapers as sources of "objective facts." Near the Lord Beresford engraving, there was a display of Zulu spears, shields, and knobberies. The exhibit text discussed the partial nature of museum collections, and the way in which these collections promote stereotypes, such as the image of the fierce Zulu warrior.

In designing the Military Hall, Cannizzo wanted to stress the "regimentation" that Europeans imposed upon African artifacts (Cannizzo 1991a: 153). Artifacts were presented as ethnographic specimens, formally organized in old-fashioned walnut cases. This subtle exploration of the artifice and effects of various exhibiting styles was further developed at the end of the Military Hall, where the visitor viewed a reconstruction of a Victorian sitting room that featured a prominent display of African weapons. Here Cannizzo wanted to communicate a sense of the life history of these weapons, particularly their redefinition as war trophies destined to be proudly displayed in a Victorian parlor (Cannizzo 1991a: 151). When I saw this display, I stood alongside two

No. 2099.—VOL. LXXV.   SATURDAY, SEPTEMBER 6, 1879.   WITH WHOLE SHEET SUPPLEMENT | SIXPENCE. By Post, 6½d.

Figure 2.2 "Lord Beresford's Encounter with a Zulu." *Illustrated London News* (1879), featured in "The Imperial Connection" installation from *Into the Heart of Africa.*

elderly women who were admiring the Victorian furniture, reminding me of the difficulty of critically re-presenting imperial ideology.

This technique of showing multiple recontextualizations of objects is reminiscent of Susan Vogel's important reflexive exhibit *Art/Artifact* (1988), which showed at the Center for African Art in New York. Like Cannizzo, Vogel is interested in questioning museological representations of Africa. The layout of *Art/Artifact* created an historical collage, depicting various ways that objects from Africa have been represented—as curiosity, as artifact, as art—by the West.

This focus on various styles of presentation in museums reflects a theoretical orientation that challenges the ideology of transparent representation that dominates natural history and anthropological museums. Rather than accept the museum's authority to present objective, neutral representations, Cannizzo stresses the way in which exhibits inevitably reflect the attitudes and assumptions of those who design them. In this sense, we become aware of the artifice and contingency of exhibiting. We are reminded of the work of culture critic James Clifford (1986), who cautions anthropologists that their texts are but "partial truths." Building on Clifford's theme, Cannizzo argues that exhibits are not neutral or "exact" representations of reality.

The third section of the exhibit, the Missionary Room, housed artifacts collected by Canadian Protestant missionaries. The room had a cruciform floor plan and white walls, which Cannizzo explains, were intended to suggest the "light" that missionaries felt they were bringing to Africa (1991a: 151). David Livingstone's words appeared on one wall: "My desire is to open a path to Central Africa that civilization, commerce and Christianity might find their way there." The language of the opening panel to the Missionary Room echoed Livingstone's words:

CIVILIZATION, COMMERCE AND CHRISTIANITY

Venture into the Heart of Africa

Inspired by the exploits of Dr. David Livingstone, several generations of Canadian missionaries followed the path opened by the Victorian hero. Their vision, like his, was to replace "paganism" with Christianity, the slave trade with legitimate commerce, and "barbarous customs" with "civilization." The sense of cultural superiority inherent in these goals and the genuine spirit of adventure which often motivated the missionaries were both characteristic of the period. Some lost their lives through their desire to bring "light" to the "Dark Continent."

This introductory panel set the context for viewing a number of artifacts collected by missionaries—who were fascinated by fetish objects and prone to collecting combs as proof of the "basic civility" of Africans—as well as reproductions of photographs taken by missionaries. Two reproductions of early twentieth-century Belgian postcards entitled "Young Bantandu Woman" and "Young Civilized Negress" proved somewhat controversial (see Figure 2.3). Some viewers found the images offensive, while others read them as interesting colonial documents. Perhaps Cannizzo's text did not properly communicate the way in which such photos were used for propaganda and for edification. On the other hand, the display did, I think, strongly suggest how humanitarian ideology can be complicit with imperialism.[11]

Cannizzo's strategy of immersing visitors in imperialist and missionary ideology was especially apparent in the case of the controversial lantern slide show entitled "In Livingstone's Footsteps." Museum visitors entered a small nook to watch this slide show. A narrator told visitors to imagine that they were in a Protestant church in Ontario around 1919. "You've come to hear the Reverend Charles Ashby talk about his trip along the Zambezi River," the narrator continued. The slides showed pictures of Victoria Falls, wildlife, "friendly natives," a "witchdoctor," "Christian schoolboys" and so on. The final slide showed a "civilized, Christian family in Africa," leading the fictional Reverend Ashby to end his show on a hopeful note. Following this slide, there was a brief disclaimer (spoken in Cannizzo's own voice), reminding visitors to appreciate the show's historical context, and to recognize the "paternalism and cultural arrogance" of missionary discourse. However, visitors who did not enter the nook at either the beginning or end of the seven minute slide show missed the verbal disclaimer.[12] It was also written on a panel, but as already mentioned, the museum-going public does not closely read label copy.

The life-sized model of the Ovimbundu Compound that made up the fourth phase of the exhibit was intended to offer a point of contrast with the earlier Victorian parlor (Cannizzo 1991a: 151). To recreate this Ovimbundu compound, designers built a thatch house within the museum, and then furnished it with "real objects from the collections" (Cannizzo 1991a: 155), providing a realist display of the domestic economy of the Ovimbundu (see Figure 2.4). The mimetic aura of this display contrasted sharply with other parts of the exhibit where Cannizzo was quite frank about the limitations of our knowledge about the artifacts on display. Labels expressed uncertainty, as in the following example:

> This statue was almost certainly made by an Igbo artist around the turn of the century, in a village in south-eastern Nigeria. We don't know what it was used for, although it is probably the representation of a spirit.

In contrast, the reproduction of the Ovimbundu Compound had an aura of closure, not unlike a still photograph. Visitors were shown the Ovimbundu compound, complete with thatched roof house, tools and weapons, a corn pounder, fish traps, wickerwork, wood and iron work, cooking and eating

Figure 2.3 "Missionary Room" installation from *Into the Heart of Africa.*

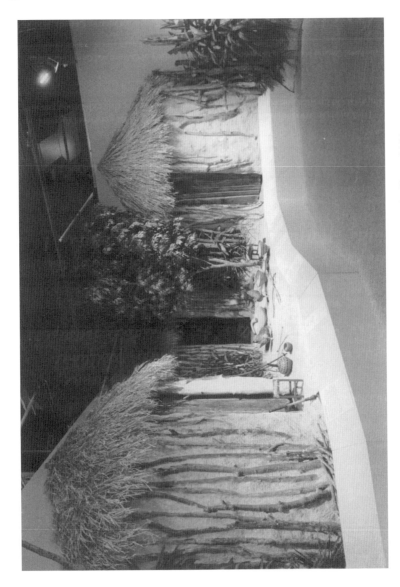

Figure 2.4 "Ovimbundu Compound" installation from *Into the Heart of Africa.*

utensils, coiled baskets, stools, and musical instruments. In one interview on African art historian challenged this representation of the Ovimbundu: "It's the mud hut stereotype" she said, explaining that "You get this impression that the Ovimbundu are people who live in mud huts, raise chickens, and grow maize along with some other agricultural products." She proceeded to relate a far different narrative about the Ovimbundu as merchants, slave traders and slave users, harvesters of rubber and wax, entrepreneurs, poly-lingual traders, and as blacksmiths. She concluded that the display of the Ovimbundu compound, juxtaposed with the Victorian parlour mentioned earlier, simply reiterated tired stereotypes: "Here's the wealthy, rich, superior Westerner, and here's the poor, downtrodden, peasant African." At the end of this interview, I remarked that the exhibit text accompanying the Ovimbundu Compound did fill in some of these details about Ovimbundu livelihood. However, I was also disturbed to realize that the introductory panel to the Ovimbundu Compound was called "Peoples of the Mist," possibly an inap-propriate play on "Gorillas of the Mist."

The final phase of the exhibit, the Africa Room, represented a major the-matic shift. Rather than focus on the history of the collection, Cannizzo shifted her attention to the African context. While the previous sections of the exhibit were anthropological and historical, the Africa Room was more con-cerned with aesthetics, and an art gallery style of presentation (see Figure 2.5). This final section of the exhibit included displays of textiles, masks, ancestral figures, and a popular, interactive "hands on" display of musical instruments. A number of anthropological themes were touched upon, including exchange, adornment, aesthetics, warfare, power and privilege, cultural rhythms, rites of passage, and ritual life. Here, promotions of *Into the Heart of Africa* as a cele-bration of African cultures and artistic traditions made sense. The tone of the exhibit was no longer ironic, but rather celebratory and respectful. For many visitors, and particularly protestors, this final section of the exhibit was satisfying, a redeeming feature of sorts. Clearly, the Africa Room appeared to respond best to CFTA demands that the ROM show the "immense contri-butions made by Africa, and by people of African heritage to humanity" (CFTA 1990: 1).

While many visitors enjoyed the beauty and the warm atmosphere of the Africa room, I suspect that Cannizzo was less enthralled by this part of the exhibit. In her earlier writing on museums, Cannizzo states that she has no interest in creating "bland, ethnic Disneyland[s] full of success stories and multicultural kiosks" (1989b: 169). Certainly, Cannizzo is not alone among curators in her frustration with traditional museum representations of celebra-tory histories and "authentic" culture (see Guedon 1983, Halpin 1983, Jones 1992). Jane Peirson Jones, a curator for *Gallery 33: A Meeting Ground of Cultures*, a permanent exhibit that opened in 1990 in the Birmingham Museum and Art Gallery, has written about this tension between critical and popular

Figure 2.5   "Africa Room" installation from *Into the Heart of Africa.*

exhibits. Jones (1992: 229) points out that while curators may want to address issues of cultural and political conflict, museum visitors may continue to desire upbeat "icons of diversity" exhibits—costumes, festivals, ethnic foods, and so on.

It is important to note that many prominent curators, including both Susan Vogel and Marjorie Halpin (both of whom Cannizzo has interviewed), regard exhibits that highlight aesthetic qualities of objects as liberating. Halpin, working at the Museum of Anthropology (MOA) in Vancouver, has analyzed the way that exhibit labels, with their urge to classify and to tell a cohesive story, detract from the primacy of objects in museums. Like Vogel, she rejects the curatorial impulse to exert strong cognitive control over the objects, and prefers to create a more phenomenological exhibit. This position clearly recognizes the problematic legacy of anthropological and natural history museums in imposing stereotypical classifications upon objects. We must release objects from their "intellectual domination," explains Halpin (1983: 268). Many native artists in Canada agree, and Michael Ames reports that these artists want to be "freed from their ethnological fate" (1991: 8). In the case of African collections, the migration of these objects from dusty ethnological museums to the privileged niche of the art gallery is a dramatic and lucrative story. Ironically, it has come about only because the West "discovered" primitive art, and employed it to subvert and remake Western artistic traditions (Clifford 1988).

In any case, the fact that *Into the Heart of Africa* was sensitive to both a cultural and aesthetic appreciation of the ROM's collection is itself unusual. It is only recently that this strict dichotomy between art and artifact, and the art gallery and the museum, has begun to break down.[13] This successful aspect of *Into the Heart of Africa* was likely facilitated by the fact that the ROM has always been a general museum, a place where "the sciences and art and archeology departments are still integrated and retained beneath one roof" (Cruise 1977: 9).

Upon leaving the Africa Room, visitors viewed an eclectic display of photographs of contemporary Africa. Cannizzo included these photographs as a way of challenging the salvage paradigm that dominates anthropological exhibits. As mentioned in the beginning of this chapter, the salvage paradigm, with its obsession with authenticity, denies the current historical situation of cultures. The West "museumifies" other cultures, effectively denying other peoples their current historical and political lives. Cannizzo displayed images of contemporary Africa—including one photo of a child in Soweto, which was one of the few (rather unthreatening) images of resistance in the entire exhibit—to counteract the museum's tendency to freeze all that it displays.

But Cannizzo's critical intentions were not always consistently presented. While the photographic gallery at the end of the exhibit provided images of contemporary Africa, promotion for *Into the Heart of Africa* appealed to our

urge to know, and appropriate, a mythical, "authentic" Africa. *Equinox* readers received the following "handwritten" invitation (see Figure 2.6) to come
to the ROM:

> Dear Equinox Reader,
>
> Have you ever wondered what it must have been like to explore unknown Africa
> over 100 years ago? Find out—take a journey INTO THE HEART OF AFRICA,
> a special exhibition at the Royal Ontario Museum from November 16, 1989 to
> July 29, 1990, highlighting the collections made by Canadian military men and
> missionaries.
>
> As you travel INTO THE HEART OF AFRICA, you'll visit a village com-
> pound, hear traditional African music and follow "In Livingstone's Footsteps"
> with a narrated lantern-slide show.
>
> I hope you'll join us for INTO THE HEART OF AFRICA—a celebration of
> the vitality of Africa's many peoples and cultures!
>
> Sincerely,
Dr. Jeanne Cannizzo
Curator

Here, the Heart of Africa has turned into an exotic, mysterious destination, so
that this invitation is much like the safari brochure from Zimbabwe mentioned earlier. Both use language that plays off a familiar primitivist discourse
where Africa is dark, dangerous, enticing, and unknown, because Westerners
are ignorant of it (Torgovnick 1990).

Given Cannizzo's intention of critiquing colonial collecting, it is also
ironic that *Into the Heart of Africa* ended with a special ROM gift shop, where
visitors could acquire their own souvenirs of Africa such as textiles, masks,
jewelry, postcards, posters, and the exhibit catalogue (see Figure 2.7).[14] Based
on these examples, it appears that *Into the Heart of Africa* both critiqued and
reproduced the politics of cultural imperialism. This ambiguity forms, I think,
an important context for considering the multiple, and complex, responses to
Into the Heart of Africa.

It is possible that Cannizzo had little control over these promotional
aspects of the exhibit. Cannizzo has noted that she and her curatorial team
(including an architect, a graphics designer, a co-ordinator, an artist, and an
interpretive planner), did have to accommodate, and negotiate with, a wide
variety of museum personnel regarding issues such as security, conservation
requirements, and visitor services. Moreover, Cannizzo writes that, "the most
difficult, and never really settled, negotiations were surely those that revolved
around the institutional subculture, the decades long praxis determined by
'custom' and 'tradition' at this particular museum" (1991a: 151). Without a
doubt, it is difficult to create an oppositional exhibit within an establishment
museum such as the ROM. Curator Christina Kreps states that museums can

INTO
THE HEART
OF
AFRICA

Dear Equinox Reader,

Have you ever wondered what it must have been like to explore unknown Africa over 100 years ago? Find out - take a journey INTO THE HEART OF AFRICA, a special exhibition at the Royal Ontario Museum from November 16, 1989 to July 29, 1990, highlighting the collections made by Canadian military men and missionaries.

As you travel INTO THE HEART OF AFRICA, you'll visit a village compound, hear traditional African music and follow "In Livingstone's Footsteps" with a narrated lantern-slide show.

I hope you'll join us for INTO THE HEART OF AFRICA - a celebration of the vitality of Africa's many peoples and cultures!

Sincerely,
Dr. Jeanne Cannizzo
Curator

The Royal Ontario Museum gratefully acknowledges the most generous support of Imperial Oil Limited and Nabisco Brands Ltd, which has made this exhibition possible.

Imperial Oil (Esso)   NABISCO BRANDS

The Royal Ontario Museum is an agency of the Ontario Ministry of Culture and Communications

ROM   Royal Ontario Museum, 100 Queen's Park, Toronto, Ontario, Canada M5S 2C6
CALL (416) 586-5549 FOR MORE INFORMATION

Photo/Mongo Dancer, Zaire, before 1930   Supplement to Equinox Magazine

Figure 2.6 Advertisement for *Into the Heart of Africa*.

Figure 2.7 Gift shop at the end of *Into the Heart of Africa.*

"transcend their [colonial] heritage and become unique forces for fostering the kind of global thinking so urgently needed in the world today" (1988: 56). She reports that the Tropenmuseum in Amsterdam is increasingly addressing issues concerning third world development. Ironically though, several board members of the research institute affiliated with this museum are managers of Dutch multinationals that have strong financial interests in developing countries.

Major museums face cutbacks in government grants, and find themselves competing with shopping malls for audiences. In this light, the turn to flashy advertising is not surprising. In his article, "Exhibiting the Imperial Image," curator Christopher Bayly has written about the difficulties of choosing a promotional image and title for the exhibit, *The Raj: India and the British 1600–1947*, which showed at the National Portrait Gallery in London (1990–91). The term "The Raj" was chosen for the title partly because it echoes Paul Scott's popular *Raj Quartet* novels, and the spin-off television series. Bayly admits that this choice was

> a necessary adjustment to the realities of running a gallery today. Visitors, of course, have to be attracted in the first place. Drier academic titles or obscurities along the lines of 'Glories of the Orient' could not be guaranteed to do this. (1991: 13)

However, although the title focused visitors' interests on British involvement in India, the exhibit did try to keep a critical edge, and to represent Indian nationalism and Muslim movements as fully as it did British imperialism. Sally Price (1989: 119–121) also describes how publicists have a tendency to exploit, rather than explain, primitivist stereotypes.

It is difficult to determine if institutional pressures greatly inhibited Cannizzo. Comments by people I interviewed who work, or worked for the ROM, all suggest that Cannizzo had an unusually high level of curatorial independence. On the other hand, institutional pressures may still have inhibited her from making a stronger critique of the museum and colonial collecting. After all, it should be noted that when the exhibit first opened, the ROM's biggest worry was that they would offend important patrons, many of whom probably donated artifacts to the collection. This may explain why, for example, there was no explicit condemnation of colonialism in the exhibit.

Institutional pressures aside, I think that the political ambiguity of *Into the Heart of Africa* was strongly shaped by Cannizzo's rather limited success in addressing the politics and processes of exhibiting. Consider, for example, Cannizzo's justification of her choice of a promotional image for *Into the Heart of Africa* (see Plate 4). The promotional image was a picture of an unnamed female dancer from Zaire, photographed by a Canadian missionary sometime before 1930. The woman's face is painted white on one side, and her expression is poignant. Cannizzo justifies the use of this haunting poster image, explaining that "it is not the more predictable 'warrior' or 'chief' of the popular mind, nor an image of a starving or destitute refugee most familiar from television news coverage of recurrent famines in Africa" (1991a: 152). This quote reveals one of Cannizzo's main intellectual and ethical concerns, which is the misrepresentation of Africa. However, her awareness of the symbolic violence of stereotypes of Africans seems limited, for she does not recognize the gendered political implications of this exotic photo. Malek Alloula's comments on colonial postcards are appropriate here. On the passivity of models in these postcards, he writes that the good model is

> without individual will and capable of infinite malleability. The initial violence inflicted by the photographer is borne, in all its consequences, by the model. Her image is never her own. (Alloula 1986: 21)

Here, we begin to understand that colonialism is, among other things, an expression of the violence of the gaze. It is not only political overrule, but also symbolic domination (Comaroff and Comaroff 1991: 15). As Alloula explains, "colonialism imposes upon the colonized society the everpresence and omnipotence of a gaze to which everything must be transparent" (1986: 31). In this light, using the picture of an anonymous female dancer to promote *Into the Heart of Africa* is problematic. Cannizzo might have used this photograph more productively had she been able to use this woman's black and white face to focus visitors' attention on the subject of colonial encounters.[15]

Interestingly, Cannizzo included material which revealed the complicity of colonial domination and photography (or representation, more generally). But she did little with it. In the Missionary Room, Cannizzo included the following statement by Canadian Reverend A. W. Banfield. Reflecting on his experience of taking photos in Africa, Banfield wrote:

> I had a hard job taking the photograph as the woman had to be held while I set up my camera. Just as soon as she was released and I had pressed the bulb, she ran away again. Poor creature, she thought I was going to kill her with that horrid looking thing, the camera.

This comment clearly reveals the unequal power relations inherent in voyeurism. As Kenneth Little comments with regard to the behavior of tourists taking photos on safari: "The camera substitutes for the gun and tourists "shoot" their pictures and "capture" images in order to make their photo albums into trophies" (1991: 156, see also O'Rourke 1987). While Cannizzo was brave to include Reverend Banfield's words in *Into the Heart of Africa*, she might have further explored explicitly the complicity between colonialism and representation. Such an analysis would lead to a different exhibit, one which would have addressed (and perhaps countered) the palpable silence of Africans in the colonial photographs displayed in *Into the Heart of Africa*.

In making this argument, I am influenced by the work of Timothy Mitchell. While Cannizzo (1991a: 151) assumes that museums "reflect" the violence of colonialism, Mitchell's analysis in *Colonising Egypt* (1988) suggests that museums actually reproduce the politics of colonialism. And while Cannizzo is rightly concerned with stereotypes and misrepresentations of Africans, Mitchell takes us a step further by focusing on the politics of the very process of exhibiting others.

Museums Will Be Museums

Mitchell argues that the West has a habit of rendering up the world as object, or, as he calls it, "the world as exhibition" (1989). This process of objectification occurs because we organize reality through forms of representation such as exhibits, models, dioramas, maps, classifications, and plans. Moreover, Mitchell argues that this process of ordering up the world is identical to colonialism's apparatus and logic, since it reflects a political will to domesticate others, both in body and mind. In *Colonising Egypt* (1988), Mitchell describes how this process played itself out in nineteenth-century Egypt. Colonial methods, such as the creation of systematized school systems, and the rebuilding and mapping of cities, rested upon a European desire to make Egypt picture-like and readable to the Western eye. Model villages were built to produce an ordered, codified space over which Europeans could exercise surveillance. In this way, the people of Egypt were made inmates of their own villages.

Interestingly, Cannizzo mentions a similar situation in her description of Canadian Reverend Walter Currie's career at Chisamba missionary station in Angola. In the exhibit catalogue, Cannizzo shows pictures of Currie's carpentry workshop and the model square homes that were designed to house nuclear families. Cannizzo comments briefly on the way in which these homes disrupted extended kin relations and emphasized the loyalty of the couple (1989a: 35). This is an interesting point, however Mitchell's analysis of the world as exhibition allows us to take it further. We need to consider not only the implications of building model homes, but also the implications of the photographs of these homes and their occupants. Mitchell's point is that these European representations—from photographs to postcards to exhibits— all contribute to the aura of political certainty that informs colonialism. In this light, the museum is not just a house for artifacts—it is a part of what Mitchell ominously calls the machinery of representation.

Mitchell's analysis clarifies the way in which museums and colonialism share a cultural logic. It becomes clear that much of *Into the Heart of Africa* reproduces the objectification and politics that Mitchell describes. Consider, for example, the promotional material mentioned earlier that asked visitors to "journey INTO THE HEART OF AFRICA" and to "explore unknown Africa". This invitation, as with safari brochures, rests upon the same desires as those of orientalist Sylvestre de Sacy, who wanted to establish a splendid museum where "students would be able to feel transported as if by enchantment into the midst of, say, a Mongolian tribe or of the Chinese race, whichever he might have made the object of his studies" (in Mitchell 1989: 220). De Sacy's writings reveal an important paradox in this process of objectification. On the one hand, the Westerner views the other from close proximity. But at the same time, a distance is constructed, the other is fixed as a silent object of both our studies and our safaris. It is this distance that allows Westerners to view others from a voyeuristic and privileged position of power.

Unfortunately, despite Cannizzo's interest in the museum as a place for dialogue and multiple narratives, *Into the Heart of Africa* did not challenge or subvert this process of objectification. Historical photographs in the exhibit showed image after image of silenced Africans, in school uniforms, in front of missionary stations, and so on. Yet Cannizzo did not demystify, or allow others to demystify, this palpable silence (Freedman 1990, Schildkrout 1991). In other words, *Into the Heart of Africa* was remarkably void of images and voices of resistance, an omission which, I think, played a major role in protestors' rejection of the exhibit. Certainly, it is not difficult to find important African responses to imperial domination. One could mention wars of resistance fought, for example, by the Zulu and Ashanti peoples, both of whom were depicted in *Into the Heart of Africa*. More importantly, responses can be found in the words and writing of leaders of the Negritude movement, and of African independence movements.

Finally, Cannizzo's style of curatorship is very much like the fieldwork style of Clifford Geertz, one of her intellectual heroes. In *Anthropology as Culture Critique*, George Marcus and Michael Fischer note that Geertz has tended to "conceive of the interpreter as being a certain distance from the object of interpretation, as a reader might engage in a text, rather than in terms of a metaphor of dialogue" (1986: 29). Similarly, Cannizzo—despite her earlier populist statements—created *Into the Heart of Africa* by following Geertz's distanced approach to interpreting culture. As noted earlier, Cannizzo has written about her experience of having discovered multiple narratives to tell the story of *Into the Heart of Africa* while she was hidden away in the ROM basement looking at artifacts. This approach to her material led Cannizzo to understand culture as a text to be deciphered, as opposed to thinking of representations of culture as an "interplay of voices" (Clifford 1986: 12) speaking to, with, against, and past each other.

Chapter III

Prelude to the Controversy

The Ambiguity of Irony

When *Into the Heart of Africa* opened in November 1989, it received favorable reviews from diverse audiences. Colin Rickards, writing for *Share*, which describes itself as "Canada's largest ethnic paper," praised the exhibit highly. He commended the ROM for showing its African collection to the public, and he described Cannizzo's reflexive approach as fascinating:

> Jeanne Cannizzo, who has worked and studied in Sierra Leone, pondered over the question of whether she could make some 350 selected objects from this Aladdin's Cave of memorabilia into an exhibition. She could, and did, and her brainchild became the Into the Heart of Africa exhibition which is currently running at the ROM. It is rapidly becoming—and rightly so—one of the most successful of the Museum's recent exhibitions.
>
> (Rickards 1989b)

Interestingly, Rickards made special note of the Lord Beresford engraving which, some months later, became a site of intense contestation. For Rickards (1989a), this engraving allowed the visitor to "see the realities of the Zulu War—from the viewpoint of the Zulus". In contrast, protestors of *Into the Heart of Africa* usually referred to the Lord Beresford engraving to make a point about, as one woman said to me, "the horrifying visual images" of the exhibit. Despite Rickards' positive comments about *Into the Heart of Africa*, *Share* eventually became an important forum for the black community to voice complaints against the ROM, as well as a forum through which the ROM later attempted to mend bridges with its black constituents.

41

The first responses to *Into the Heart of Africa* by allies and families of missionaries were also remarkably positive compared with later accusations that the ROM had presented negative stereotypes of missionaries. Arnold Edinborough, writing for the *Anglican Journal*, called the exhibit a "gentle triumph" (1989). His review is interesting in that it revealed no indication that missionary discourses were critiqued in *Into the Heart of Africa*. He repeated the language of the exhibit, but his tone was nostalgic and aggrandizing rather than critical. Consider, for example, Edinborough's description of Rev. Walter T. Currie: "Even when [Rev. Currie] was on furlough in 1903, rather than come home he retraced the steps of Livingstone, traveling some 1000 miles or more through the heart of the continent".

The fact that Edinborough did not appear to be unsettled by *Into the Heart of Africa* is indicative of the exhibit's political and semiotic ambivalence discussed in the previous chapter. For successful irony *is* unsettling. As Richard Rorty, in *Contingency, Irony and Solidarity* argues, irony's power is based on redescribing our "final vocabularies" (1989: 73). Thus, an ironist understands that our language, conscience, and communities are contingent and fallible, the product of history. Rorty situates this awareness of the contingency of our deepest beliefs in the historical context of the French Revolution, the Romantics, and Nietzsche. With the social upheaval of the French Revolution, he suggests, it became possible to imagine that we make our world and our truths. Following 1789, the Romantic poets taught us that we could change our world through the creation of new metaphors and language. Before the Romantics, artists followed classical, coded conventions, rather than seek to create new language. This growing sense of our own contingency was articulated by Nietzsche who wrote that truth is a "mobile army of metaphors" (in Rorty 1989: 17).

We live with this sense of contingency, Rorty says, once we reach "the point where we no longer worship anything, where we treat nothing as a quasi divinity" (1989: 22). Clearly, such a world view would appear unsettling to a missionary who believes in a religious truth. Following Rorty's account of the ironist's sensibility, we have every reason to predict that missionaries and their allies might feel disempowered by Cannizzo's ironic presentation of missionary discourse (indeed many did).[1] But this was not the case for Edinborough, who instead stressed that *Into the Heart of Africa* was an exhibit that spoke to timeless, universal themes: "Here we have objects which take us into the hearts of men and women of whatever color in whatever country in whatever age. A gentle triumph that, for the Royal Ontario Museum" (1989: 17). Edinborough's reading is indicative of the exhibit's political ambiguity, but also reflects the fact that no curator can control the meaning of her exhibit. In a CBC *Ideas* program on museums, Cannizzo makes this point by employing the metaphor of the museum as theater: "The museum doesn't present just one play, it presents as many plays as there are visitors.

Because I think that the visitors are the playwrights and the directors and the audience as well" (1989: 23). In contrast to Edinborough's reading of the exhibit, such mainstream publications as the *Globe and Mail* and the *Toronto Star* appreciated the critical tone of *Into the Heart of Africa*, and depicted the exhibit as being theoretically on the cutting edge. Christopher Hume, writing for the *Toronto Star*, appreciated the way the exhibit examined collectors as well as the collection:

> Ten, even five years ago, a show like this would simply have been a celebration of African tribal arts and crafts. But now the baskets, masks, spears and jewelry are balanced by displays devoted to the soldiers and missionaries who collected the artifacts and the context in which they operated. (1989: E3)

Similarly, Adele Freedman, in her article "A revealing journey through time and space" (1989), presented *Into the Heart of Africa* as an innovative, challenging exhibit. She quoted David Fujiwara, an architect who was a part of Cannizzo's curatorial team, as saying, "It's as far as we could push the ethnographic museum in 1989." Concluding her article with a vision of a future with radically different museums, or perhaps no museums at all, Freedman wrote:

> Come the revolution, should these artifacts still be at the ROM, should there still be a ROM, there would be no such thing as pedestals and cases. A person might be able to touch the objects, play with them. But even for a spectator to express such a wish is part of Cannizzo's plan.

While the above reviews recognized Cannizzo's reflexive intentions, other articles reiterated, in an unselfconscious fashion, the primitivist tropes and imperialist ideology that Cannizzo presented ironically. One article in *Key to Toronto*, entitled "Out of Africa" (echoing Isak Dinesen's *Out of Africa*), had a sub-heading that read: "After many years of cultivation and exploration, the Royal Ontario Museum sheds new light on the Dark Continent."[2] This article described the exhibit as an exploration of the "various economic, political and cosmological structures within the Dark Continent." It also noted that collecting by soldiers and missionaries had aided the ROM in "nurturing a highly sophisticated collection of artifacts," thus valorizing, rather than challenging, colonial collecting. In a similar vein, another article noted that Reverend Banfield's English Nupe Bible holds "an honored place in the ROM's 'Into the Heart of Africa' exhibition, exemplifying the kind of commitment and determination shown by Canadian missionaries."[3]

These readings of *Into the Heart of Africa* illustrate how irony is politically ambiguous since it works within and against a dominant tradition. Cannizzo's irony, for example, depends upon self-consciously appropriating and undermining existing images and rhetoric such as "dark continent" or "spoils of war." This strategy reminds us of Linda Hutcheon's evaluation of postmodernism as an ironic and reflexive mode that is "rather like saying something whilst at the same time putting inverted commas around what is being said" (1989: 1). For Hutcheon, irony (and more generally, postmodernism), risks being a "complicitous critique" (1989: 2). Irony both subverts and reinforces the very conventions it challenges. The political ambiguity and unintended readings of Cannizzo's irony meant that missionaries could view *Into the Heart of Africa* with "innocent" nostalgia, while the CFTA accused Cannizzo of romanticizing Livingstone. The CFTA pamphlet reads: "It is folly to state or suggest that invaders such as Dr. Livingstone were heros of the African people" (1990: 2). Both groups missed Cannizzo's understated irony.

Newspaper articles that highlighted the exhibit's exotic tourist appeal also undermined Cannizzo's reflexive intentions. Newspaper headlines invited readers to "explore the heart of Africa" and to take an "exotic trip into [the] Heart of Africa."[4] Here, Africa is once again a Western projection, despite Cannizzo's interest in rendering primitivist tropes problematic.

Despite differences in interpretation, all of these early reviews supported *Into the Heart of Africa*, so that the exhibit's success and Cannizzo's curatorial authority appeared to be uncontested. However, even before the exhibit opened, Cannizzo and the ROM had received complaints about the exhibit. The seeds of the controversy were in place a considerable time before *Into the Heart of Africa* opened.

Power Relations and Public Culture

Months before *Into the Heart of Africa* opened, the ROM hired Sandra Whiting, a publicist from the black community, to review the exhibit's promotional materials. She voiced concerns about both the images and language used in the brochure, concerns that the ROM soon heard from other people who had obtained copies of the brochure. In April 1989, a teacher named Elizabeth Parchment brought the brochure to the attention of Hari Lalla, a Toronto Board of Education Curriculum Advisor on issues related to Race Relations and Multiculturalism. Because Toronto Board students and teachers would be invited to the exhibit, Lalla and Parchment sought a meeting with Cannizzo and her curatorial team in order to discuss what they saw as the "alarming content of the brochure" (Lalla and Myers 1990: 6). At this point, the brochure began:

> Africa. Birthplace of humanity, still a continent of mystery to many. A little over 100 years ago, as part of the scramble for African colonies, Canadian military men and missionaries set out to help conquer and convert the peoples of that unexplored territory for the British Empire. What would it have been like to travel into the unknown with these Victorian explorers, soldiers and missionaries?

Join us for a journey Into the Heart of Africa, a special exhibition at the Royal Ontario Museum that offers a unique opportunity to see the ROM's outstanding African collection.

The brochure also pointed out that the African art on display "reveals almost as much about the Canadian collector as it does about the African creator," and that exhibit visitors would have the opportunity to "follow 'In Livingstone's Footsteps' with a narrated lantern-slide show from missionary archives" (see Plate 2).

In his contribution to a joint report (Lalla and Myers 1990) on the exhibit, Lalla expressed a number of concerns regarding its promotion, many of which coalesced around issues concerning irony, stereotypes, and perspective. For example, Lalla pointed out that the exhibit did not contextualize its ironic use of missionary and colonizer's discourse, an omission that meant that students, as well as many adults, would not understand the exhibit's irony. Such misunderstandings would occur, Lalla predicted, "particularly if the literal reading [of the exhibit text] conforms to a previously held biased view, subtle or otherwise." Further, Lalla noted that people with a less developed knowledge of grammar might interpret the exhibit quotation marks to be an authoritative acknowledgment of sources, of "truths about Africa that are in fact not truths at all" (1990: 3). In fact this is a common way to read quotation marks. To complicate things further, Cannizzo used quotation marks in multiple ways, so that they needed to be read literally and ironically, and above all, contextually.

With regard to the promotional image of the Mongo woman in a grass-skirt, Lalla pointed out that it had no relation to the exhibit's intended critical perspective. Rather, the image invited "viewers to a biased perception of primitives and other *National Geographic*-like images of Africa" (1990: 4). Indeed, the idea of museums as spaces for critical engagement and dialogue is often undermined by the tendency to highlight the exotic. This is a part of a broad cultural practice that exists beyond the walls of museums. In his article "The Third Space," Homi Bhabha describes how "the sign of the 'cultured' or the 'civilized' attitude is the ability to appreciate cultures in a kind of *musée imaginaire*; as though one should be able to collect and appreciate them" (1990: 208). But, as Bhabha shows, this focus on cultural diversity and exotica occurs in lieu of a recognition of histories of dispossession, difference, and domination. In a similar vein, Catherine Lutz and Jane Collins (1993: 59–61) show how the "timeless" values of universalism and humanism inform the popular travel magazine *National Geographic*, which might be seen as a portable museum. Finally, Lalla's most general concern focused on the perspective of the exhibit, which, he suggested, valorized the lives of Canadian collectors over those of African artists.

Lalla and Parchment expressed these concerns to Cannizzo and two members of her staff at a private meeting held in May 1989. After the meeting, Lalla and Parchment felt that they had received some assurances that their suggestions for changes to the brochure, and to the exhibit, would be considered.

On June 28, 1989, the ROM held a reception for selected leaders of the black community to introduce them to the exhibit. Neither Lalla nor Parchment were invited to this reception, an omission which did not impress Lalla. Included in a package of documents that he gave to me, was a rather tardy letter of apology (dated December 8, 1989) from the ROM. In fact, the ROM's choice of community leaders was viewed by many critics and protestors as highly strategic, with the ROM predictably choosing successful community leaders. Rico, a member of the CFTA, who is Rastafarian, made this point to me by noting, with some sarcasm: "I am not on the ROM's list of community leaders." (I doubt, however, that Rico and many other CFTA members would accept a position with the ROM.)

Although Lalla and Parchment were not present at the ROM's reception, others among the fifty guests had obtained copies of the exhibit's promotional brochure. The reception was reported in the alternative press, and its tense atmosphere was described by curator Hazel Da Breo in the winter issue of *Fuse* magazine. At the reception, Cannizzo and Lewis Levine, the Associate Director of Exhibitions, introduced the exhibit and its promotional materials. Da Breo describes Levine as having been "patronizing and insensitive" (1989/90: 33), and she recalls the shock and anger that guests felt upon realizing that the exhibit was a "fait accompli." The guests felt that they had been invited to rubber stamp the exhibit, as opposed to being able to offer substantial critiques and suggestions. Da Breo describes how this power dynamic alienated the guests, making them feel excluded from public culture. One protestor expressed this sense of frustration to me by saying: "We are taxpayers too. We should also be the beneficiaries."

While the ROM carefully orchestrated the reception, it did not go as smoothly as planned. Da Breo describes the ROM staff during the reception as having acted like "dinosaurs ... clumsily lumbering through unfamiliar territory" (1989/90: 34). This description of the ROM staff illustrates how, as Kondo (1990: 45) observes, "those who have power are caught in power relations even as they dominate others". Given this, it would be reductionist to think of the conflict at the ROM as a Manichean struggle between the powerful and the powerless. Power works in a far more intricate and ambivalent fashion (Bhabha 1990: 220). Finally, although the reception was intended to welcome members of the black community to the ROM (it was even held in the prestigious members' lounge), it appeared to establish and entrench an opposition between the museum professionals and the museum's black constituency. This relationship reiterated the symbolic basis of colonial domination described by Jean and John Comaroff as

> the act of conceptualizing, inscribing, and interacting with ["others"] on terms not of their choosing; in making them into the pliant objects and silenced

subjects of our scripts and scenarios; in assuming the capacity to "represent" them. (1991: 15)

The issue of course, is whether or not an establishment museum can diffuse or subvert its own power and privilege. Can museums be decolonized? I will return to these larger questions in my Afterword. Meanwhile, let us continue to examine how the ROM "managed" its difficult situation.

The Politics of Consultation

Immediately after the reception, the ROM hired Woods Gordon Management Consultants to organize focus groups to discuss the exhibit brochure and strategies for marketing the exhibit (Crawford, Hankel and Rowse 1990: 10). Two focus groups of eight people each were established. The first group was formed from the guest list of the reception, while the second group was made up of other people considered to be leaders of the black community of Toronto. Both focus groups debated the merits and problems of the brochure, and came to a consensus that its language was negative and stereotypical. Most participants felt that the brochure should be rewritten, a proposition that the ROM took up, at a cost of approximately $28,000 (Fulford 1991: 22). The revised brochure (see Plate 3) began:

> Africa. Birthplace of humanity. A continent of ancient civilizations and complex cultures. Into the Heart of Africa, a special exhibition at the Royal Ontario Museum, invites you on an historical journey through the world of sub-Saharan Africa, illustrated by the ROM's outstanding collections.
> The rich cultural heritage of African religious, social and economic life is celebrated through objects brought back by Canadian missionaries and military men over 100 years ago. The exhibition examines this turbulent but little-known period in history when Canadians participated in Britain's efforts to colonize and convert the African nations.

We can note significant changes from the original brochure. Africa is no longer described as a "continent of mystery" and the invitation to travel with Victorian explorers, soldiers, and missionaries is downplayed. Rather, the focus of the journey is now Africa itself. This overall shift in focus is clear if we compare the last lines of the original and revised brochure. The original brochure concluded:

> Offering fascinating insight into Canada's imperial past, Into the Heart of Africa is also a thought-provoking celebration of the vitality of Africa's many peoples.

In contrast, the revised brochure reverses the order of this sentence, so that the subject of Africa is stated before that of imperialism:

> Into the Heart of Africa offers insight into the thriving vitality of Africa's many peoples, while uncovering a seldom-remembered aspect of Canadian history.

Ironically, members of the CFTA later critiqued *Into the Heart of Africa* on the basis that it did not follow this new brochure. As the CFTA stated in their pamphlet:

> The ROM is currently presenting an exhibit entitled "Into the Heart of Africa." An exhibit, which according to the ROM, is a portrayal of African history. Yet the exhibit represents a clear and concise attempt to mislead the public and to further tarnish the image of Africa and African people. (1990: 1)[5]

Expectations that the exhibit was primarily a "portrayal of African history" may have also been nurtured by the fact that the phrase "heart of Africa" is often associated with the idea of pilgrimage and authenticity. Eddy Harris, for example, has recently written a travelogue entitled *Native Stranger: A Black American's Journey Into the Heart of Africa* (1992). Here, the "heart of Africa" evokes a sense of roots, of returning home. This might partly explain why some people who came to see *Into the Heart of Africa* expected to find an "authentic" and authoritative exhibit about Africa. There is, after all, a strong tradition in North America of blacks (including Malcolm X) making pilgrimages to Africa. A number of people I interviewed referred to past travels, or planned journeys, to Africa.

Aside from critiquing the content of the brochure, a major point of contention for the focus groups was the process by which the brochure and exhibit had been created. Clearly, participants judged the consultation process to be one of eleventh-hour damage control rather than meaningful consultation. This reaction suggests that a consultation process can easily be perceived, or used, as a disciplinary tool. In fact, as resistance towards the brochure escalated, the ROM increasingly attempted to gain the approval of people judged to be representative of the black community. The logic of such a consultation process is not unlike the curator's process of exhibiting culture: in both instances a particular person or object is taken to represent the whole, whether this be an imagined whole culture, or an imagined whole community. Protestors also worked within, rather than against this logic, when they claimed that they were the true representatives of the black or the multicultural community. For instance, in response to media depictions of the CFTA as a group of militant university students, Rico stated that "a cross-section of people demonstrated at the ROM. It would make any mosaic look like a joke. There were rich white people, poor white people, some rich black people, some poor black people, Muslims, Jews, black Jews, Catholics."

On a constructive note, the focus groups suggested that the ROM involve members of the black community in an advisory capacity to aid in planning and promoting *Into the Heart of Africa*. In response to this suggestion, the ROM hired African historian Abdu Kasozi in September 1989. Employed by the ROM's Programs Department, Kasozi's role was to co-ordinate special

events such as films, lectures, and performances, to be presented in conjunc-
tion with *Into the Heart of Africa*. In preparing programs, Kasozi consulted
with three organizations that he considered to be fairly representative of the
black community in Toronto. These were the Black Secretariat, the Canadian
African Newcomer Aid Centre for Toronto, and the Jamaican Canadian
Association. While Kasozi was obviously committed to including the input of
a broad base of people in the programming, he was not unaware of the problem (both theoretical and practical) of assuming the existence of a monolithic
black community. In good particularist style, Kasozi pointed out to the ROM
that he had obtained the "consensus of the major mainstream black organizations" but that it was not at all certain that "all groups in the black community
subscribed to one view or would respect a generally agreed consensus" (in
Crawford, Hankel and Rowse 1990: 12–13). We might be tempted to say that
in hiring Kasozi, the ROM moved toward allowing for community participation in the exhibit. However, as Andrea Arbic (1991: 48) has pointed out,
Kasozi's work was limited to the domain of programming, an area that curators typically perceive to be "content soft," and therefore more amenable to
community participation. Despite hiring Kasozi, the ROM upheld its curatorial authority. This strategy of limited community participation was stated
explicitly to the media by Diane Kenyon, a spokesperson for the ROM:

> It is not "standard practice" to have the decision-making involvement of out-
> siders. We have done outreach on programs surrounding exhibits and galleries but
> the content of any exhibit is the responsibility of the academic staff at the ROM.
> (in Nazareth 1990: 11)

Kasozi co-ordinated a program of over 70 special events including lectures, music and dance performances, films, videos, community events, and
workshops. The ROM cinema devoted its winter program to showing African
films, beginning with work by Westerners in Africa, and leading up to
African productions. Videos of African history included Basil Davidson's
eight-part "Story of Africa" and Ali Mazuri's nine-part video entitled "The
Africans: A Triple Heritage." A number of shorter ethnographic and historical films about sub-Saharan Africa were also shown. Community programs
were presented by members of Canadian-African Associations in the Toronto
area, and included activities such as storytelling, singing, dancing, music,
arts, and fashion shows. The titles of the lectures were as follows: "Africa
around us"; "Ali Muzrui on Africa's Contribution to World Civilization";
"The Music of Africa"; "Openly Loved, Secretly Feared: Images of Women
in an African Society"; and "Confessions of a Curator—The Making of Into
the Heart of Africa." There was also a separate lecture series entitled "Africa
and World Civilization." Finally, there was even a contest to win a trip to
Kenya, courtesy of the African Safari Club.

The scope of this public programming was impressive. Its focus on African history and ethnography, and on contemporary artistic productions, appeared to fill in a gap where *Into the Heart of Africa* was weak. Attendance at the public programming events was approximately 8000 people. However, the public programing was not entirely successful, since it too became tainted by the political crisis surrounding *Into the Heart of Africa*. The Toronto-based Usafiri Drum and Dance Ensemble declined an invitation to perform at the ROM on May 13, 1990, as a sign of protest against the exhibit. In a letter to *Share*, Vivian Scarlett, the group's Artistic Director, stated:

> Missionaries and soldiers were a destructive part of the growth and existence of African people. [Into the Heart of Africa] continues to display the racist myths and lies that have been told for many years. We are a people proud of our heritage and culture. We will never support an exhibit that promotes racism and race hatred. (1990)

Some members of the CFTA also dismissed the ROM's public programming, viewing it as a cynical attempt to compensate for the exhibit. In a unique response, Rico questioned the "authenticity" of the performers: "There could be a challenge to the authenticity to some of these dancers, because there were groups from over here [North America] that were dancing." Similarly: "What you're hearing here would not be ancient poetry, but poetry that these people have learned since they came here." This perspective reflects Rico's valorization of black Africa (especially Ethiopia) as a site of cultural authenticity.[6] Interestingly, the lecture series on "Africa and World Civilization" and Cannizzo's lecture entitled "Confessions of a Curator" were both canceled due to lack of registration. It is difficult to determine whether the controversy played a role in these cancellations, but it is ironic that "Africa and World Civilization" appeared to respond to the CFTA's interests.

Finally, the focus groups appear to have done little to appease concerns expressed by members of the black community about *Into the Heart of Africa*. The unintended consequences of these focus groups included the creation of a high degree of suspicion of the ROM, along with the opportunity for people to come together and critically examine the brochure images. In retrospect, critics of the exhibit did not consider their participation in the focus groups to have been meaningful. As Ayanna Black said to *NOW* in March 1990 when the protests of the exhibit began: "We were concerned about the texts accompanying the exhibits and how the show was going to be laid out, but we weren't given any say in the matter" (in Nazareth 1990: 11). Similar disillusionment and anger is expressed by CFTA member Afua Cooper in her poem entitled "The Power of Racism":

> The power of racism
> the power of racism

the power of racism
is such that Neville who is six foot two and weighs 210
could be threatened with assault by three white children

The power of racism
the power of racism
the power of racism
is such that a Yusef Hawkins was killed in Brooklyn
due to the color of his skin

The power of racism
the power of racism
the power of racism is such
that the ROM could mount an African exhibition
without consulting Black people.

(1992: 73)

In summary, when *Into the Heart of Africa* opened in November 1989, members of the black community were concerned about the content of the exhibit, as well as suspicious of the ROM. This double exclusion—from the exhibit and the institution—formed the political impetus of the CFTA.[7]

Plate 1   Asante gold necklace in the introductory room of *Into the Heart of Africa*.

INTO
THE HEART
OF
AFRICA

Historical photographs, period drawings and over 300 artifacts bring
an earlier Africa to life. The intimacy of
domestic life is glimpsed in carefully woven
baskets, while powerful masks reveal the
intensity of spiritual belief. The weapons of
war and the hunt compete for our attention
with carved combs and colourful beadwork.
These objects helped shape the vision of the
continent and her peoples. From the intricate
design of an Asante gold necklace to the
simple, clean lines of Mangbetu pottery, each
piece embodies superb African artistry —
and each reveals almost as much about the
Canadian collector as it does about the
African creator.

As you travel Into The Heart
of Africa, you'll visit a village
compound in Angola, learn
how West Coast traders used
gold dust as currency, sample
the musical traditions of East
and Central Africa, and follow
"In Livingstone's Footsteps"

with a narrated lantern-slide show from
missionary archives.

Africa. Birthplace of humanity, still a
continent of mystery to many. A little
over 100 years ago, as part of the scramble
for African colonies, Canadian military men
and missionaries set out to help conquer
and convert the peoples of that unexplored
territory for the British Empire.

What would it have been like to travel into
the unknown with these Victorian explorers,
soldiers and missionaries? Join us for a journey Into The Heart of Africa, a special exhibition at the Royal Ontario Museum that
offers a unique opportunity to see the ROM's
outstanding African collection.

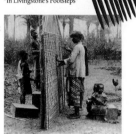

At the end of your journey,
you'll see something of contemporary Africa — an Africa with
strong links to ancestral traditions after
centuries of dramatic cultural change.

Offering fascinating insight into
Canada's imperial past, Into The
Heart of Africa is also a thought-
provoking celebration of the vitality
of Africa's many peoples.

Plate 2   Original *Into the Heart of Africa* brochure.

INTO
THE HEART
OF
AFRICA

As you travel **Into the Heart of Africa**, you'll visit a village compound in Angola, learn how West Coast traders used gold dust as currency, delight in the musical traditions of East and Central Africa and watch a narrated slide show, "In Livingstone's Footsteps," created from missionary archival materials.

Historical photographs, period drawings and over 300 artifacts bring Africa's past to life. The intimacy of domestic life in Africa is reflected in carefully woven baskets, while powerful masks reveal the intensity of spiritual belief. The weapons of war and the hunt compete for your attention with delicately carved combs and colourful beadwork. From the intricate design of an Asante gold necklace to the simple, clean lines of Mangbetu pottery, each piece embodies superb African artistry.

Africa. Birthplace of humanity. A continent of ancient civilizations and complex cultures. **Into the Heart of Africa**, a special exhibition at the Royal Ontario Museum, invites you on an historical journey through the world of sub-Saharan Africa, illustrated by the ROM's outstanding collections.

The rich cultural heritage of African religious, social and economic life is celebrated through objects brought back by Canadian missionaries and military men over 100 years ago. The exhibition examines this turbulent but little-known period in history when Canadians participated in Britain's efforts to colonize and convert the African nations.

Your journey includes highlights of contemporary Africa — a modern Africa with strong ties to ancestral traditions after centuries of dramatic change. Special lectures, films and performances will voice the spirit of Africa today.

Into the Heart of Africa offers insight into the thriving vitality of Africa's many peoples, while uncovering a seldom-remembered aspect of Canadian history.

Plate 3   Revised *Into the Heart of Africa* brochure.

Plate 4 Promotional image for *Into the Heart of Africa.*

Chapter IV

The Coalition for the Truth about Africa:
Strategies and Challenges

Performance and Resistance

In discussing the Coalition for the Truth about Africa (CFTA), I want to emphasize theoretical issues such as performance, power, resistance, and process. These concepts are useful for understanding people as agents or subjects in their own history. In a broad sense, anthropologists focus on performance in order to explain relationships between human action and the enduring social structure. What is the lasting impact, for example, when protestors demonstrate against the ROM and *Into the Heart of Africa*? The anthropology of performance stresses the productive aspect of such an encounter, focusing on how the protestors contested and redefined dominant symbols.[1] In this sense, culture is not a thing to be exhibited, but rather a "meaningful way of being in the world" (Kondo 1990: 300). Considering that museums are sites where images of the "self" and the "other" are articulated, it is not surprising that they can become focal points for struggles over defining the shape of public culture. It is no exaggeration to say that the protests of *Into the Heart of Africa* addressed large questions such as how public culture and knowledge are defined and controlled in a multicultural context like Toronto.

Victor Turner (1986) and Barbara Myerhoff (1987) both stress the potential of performance to generate reflection upon and resistance to the status quo. Through performance, or the witnessing of it, people are able to critically evaluate "the way society handles history" (Turner 1986: 22)—that is, the stories we tell about ourselves to ourselves. Many people with whom I spoke described the CFTA as having created an awareness about racism, inequity, and Eurocentrism. Even people who did not align themselves with the CFTA tended to credit the protestors with this achievement.

There is, however, a danger in romanticizing performances of resistance. Kondo (1990) raises this issue in her work on Japanese factory workers. In developing her "poststructuralist" perspective on resistance, Kondo draws upon and critiques James Scott's seminal work on peasant resistance in Malaysia, *Weapons of the Weak* (1985). I agree with Kondo's assessment that Scott's work "argues for an actor-centered, meaning-centered account of everyday acts of resistance, emphasizing the refusal of 'the poor' to accept definitions of reality imposed from above" (1990: 219). Many scholars have been able to fruitfully apply Scott's concepts of everyday resistance to a wide variety of settings. Without diminishing the importance of Scott's work, Kondo's criticism of *Weapons of the Weak* is germane to my work on the CFTA and *Into the Heart of Africa*. Kondo criticizes Scott for working with "problematic notions of categorization and human agency" (1990: 219). Scott divides Malaysian peasant society into two distinct groups, the rich and the poor. Based on her work in Japanese factories, Kondo argues that social groups do not divide themselves so neatly, as if borders were without ambiguity, tensions, and crossing points. This observation is relevant to my fieldwork experiences, where people often described multiple subject-positions with regard to the controversy. For instance, Tara Chadwick, an anthropology student I interviewed, was working at the ROM during *Into the Heart of Africa*. One lunch hour, she removed her ROM identification and spoke to members of the CFTA. Her experience of crossing this boundary was perhaps made more profound by the fact that she is of Caribbean descent and shares concerns with members of the CFTA about racism and Eurocentrism. At the same time, she did not feel entirely comfortable with the CFTA's analysis of *Into the Heart of Africa*. Many ideas about the politics of representation that she articulated with regard to the CFTA and the ROM continue to guide her own process of self-fashioning.

Kondo's second point about human agency refers to Scott's tendency to romanticize resistance, underestimating its complexity and contradictions. Kondo notes that people often find themselves

> caught in contradictions, that they simultaneously resist and reproduce, challenging and reappropriating meanings as they also undermine those challenges. That people inevitably participate in their own oppressions, buying into hegemonic ideologies even as they struggle against those oppressions and those ideologies— a familiar fact of life to women, to people of color, colonized and formerly colonized people—is a poignant and paradoxical facet of human life .... (1990: 221)

This observation speaks to my sense of the nuances and contradictions that characterized the protests of *Into the Heart of Africa*. For example, at the same time that protestors spoke against racism, they also invoked categories of race by claiming that only black people could represent black history. And while the protestors can be described as victims of racism, they also intimidated and harassed Cannizzo when she taught at the University of Toronto. This ambiguous state of affairs ensured that *Into the Heart of Africa* was never simply a debate between blacks and whites, or between the left and right. Rather, as we shall see, issues around race, class, and gender intersected with the politics of representation in complex ways.

Finally, I agree with Barbara Kirshenblatt-Gimblett's suggestion that the anthropology of performance is especially useful for studying issues such as "diversity, pluralism, cultural equity, and empowerment" (1990: 431). But as I proceed in this theoretical direction, I want to stress the importance of appreciating complexities, contradictions, and tensions within performances. Thus, rather than characterize the CFTA as speaking "the truth about unjust rule" (Turner 1977: 42), I want to understand the CFTA in a more nuanced fashion, appreciating their discourse as strategic and contingent, and as "subject to the continuous 'play' of history, culture, and power" (Hall 1992: 225, see also Gilroy 1987: 149).

The Politics of Contestation

On March 10, 1990, the CFTA held its first Saturday protest outside of the ROM, a practice that continued until *Into the Heart of Africa* closed in August 1990 (see Figure 4.1). The protests intensified on April 14, 1990, when demonstrators entered the ROM and blocked entrances and exits to the exhibits. The ROM used police assistance to move the demonstration outside. This pattern of protest and removal occurred again on April 21, 1990, with the ROM warning protestors that "entry was an offence contrary to the *Trespass to Property Act.*" On May 5, 1990, the confrontation between the CFTA and the ROM (and the police) escalated again.[2] A ROM news release dated May 11, 1990, described the confrontation:

> A number of demonstrators entered the Museum building and, after being informed that their entry was prohibited, assaulted the attending police officers and security staff of the Museum. As a result of this conduct, two individuals were charged with assaulting police officers.

Mainstream media reported these events by focusing on the violence of the clashes and printing headlines such as: "ROM demo turns ugly" and "Cops Hurt: 2 held after ROM battle."[3] This focus on violence is typical of mainstream media (Ginsburg 1989: 52), and it played a role in constructing the CFTA as militant. The fact that the newspaper headlines imitated the ROM's news release in stressing that the police were "assaulted" by protestors,

Figure 4.1 Protestors outside the Royal Ontario Museum. Photo by David Maltby.

confirmed for many members of the CFTA that the media were not on their side. But we should not assume that the protestors were complete victims in this scenario, powerless to shape or affect the situation. Newspaper photographs of white police confronting black protestors reinforced the latter's "moral power" (Dyck 1985: 190), especially in the context of Toronto's recent history of a disproportionate number of shootings of blacks by police.[4] Before considering the wider significance of these confrontations with the police, it is useful to consider CFTA reactions to *Into the Heart of Africa*, as well as the CFTA pamphlet entitled "The Truth About Africa."

Experiences of "Otherness"

Many CFTA members experienced a profound sense of denigration—a sense of being rendered "primitive" and "without history"—while visiting *Into the Heart of Africa*. For instance, Rico's memory of the exhibit was dominated by images of Africa as a "primitive" and domesticated site. He referred to the Victorian sitting room as "the trophy room," and compared its African masks to "the head of a deer or a moose on the wall." He also found the Ovimbundu compound particularly disturbing:

> It gave you a very sad feeling. The hut looked very dark inside like, uh, I don't know it was eerie, that's the word to describe it. A very eerie sort of looking place .... It reduced it to something rejectable that you wouldn't want to claim.

In expressing his disappointment, Rico graphically compared the Ovimbundu compound to a "Beresford sword through which I have no protection with I shield. Just penetrating into I heart." Deeply mistrustful of the ROM, he concluded that there was a "racist vein" running through the exhibit.

The CFTA pamphlet made similar conclusions. For instance, in response to a photograph of missionary Mrs. Thomas Titcombe giving Yagba women "a lesson in how to wash clothes" (exhibit text), the CFTA pamphlet stated:

> the depiction states that this is a scene of a white woman supervising the washing of four black women. Did Africans not know how to wash before the arrival of Europeans? There are also implicit and explicitly, subliminal and obvious statements and suggestions of Europeans civilizing and developing Africa. Terms like "Savage" and "Dark Continent" are buzzwords of this sad and disgraceful presentation. (CFTA 1990: 1)

Clearly, the CFTA did not read *Into the Heart of Africa* as critical of primitivist tropes or imperial ideology.[5] In response to the photograph of Mrs. Titcombe, their pamphlet stated:

> What should have been made clear was that the role of the missionaries, like that of the soldiers, was to be agents of the Crown. The Crown was acting on the

behalf of the colonial industry. In short, the Holy Trinity in Africa, no disrespect intended, was made up, not of the "Father, Son, and Holy Ghost," but instead, "The Missionary, Mercenary, and Merchant." (CFTA 1990: 2)

Ironically, Cannizzo intended to communicate this aspect of complicity between missionary projects and colonization, using such subtitles as "Civilization, Commerce, Christianity" to suggest these links. In contrast, CFTA members tended to read *Into the Heart of Africa* as endorsing imperial discourses about "the other."

The extent to which CFTA members associated *Into the Heart of Africa* with primitivist tropes was demonstrated to me when people I interviewed mistakenly conflated the exhibit's title with Conrad's *Heart of Darkness* (1902). One protestor referred to the exhibit as "Into the Dark Heart of Africa." Later, this protestor reviewed a transcript of our interview and realized that she had mistaken the name of the exhibit. She struck out "Into the Dark Heart of Africa" and replaced it with "Into the Heart of Darkness." Similarly, journalist Dwight Whylie (who was critical of *Into the Heart of Africa*, but not a member of the CFTA), referred to the exhibit title as "Into the Heart of Darkness."

In both of these cases, the people I spoke with referred to "Into the Heart of Darkness" while describing to me what they saw as the exhibit's negative portrayal of Africa.[6] The title, "Into the Heart of Darkness" conveyed for them this negativity, and represents a use of Conrad's *Heart of Darkness* that is not unusual. Consider, for example, how the phrase "heart of darkness" creeps into anthropologist Nancy Scheper-Hughes' description of post-colonial Brazil. Scheper-Hughes describes her fieldwork site as a "Brazilian heart of darkness" (in Hrdy 1992: 11). In a similar vein, Marianna Torgovnick (1990: 128) points out that the influential art critic William Rubin uses Conrad's title as a shorthand way of referring to a "savagery" that is assumed to be non-Western. Writing about the influence of African art on Picasso's "Les demoiselles d'Avignon" Rubin states:

> These "African" faces express more, I believe, than just the "barbaric" character of pure sexuality .... They finally conjure something that transcends our sense of civilized experience, something ominous and monstrous such as Conrad's Kurtz discovered in the heart of darkness.

Here, "heart of darkness" takes on its popular association as a site of disorder, chaos, and suffering—civilization's antithesis.

These everyday uses of the phrase "heart of darkness" are rarely cognizant of the self-conscious way that Conrad employed the term. The ambivalent nature of Conrad's *Heart of Darkness* is stressed by Christopher Miller (1985), Edward Said (1993a), and Marianna Torgovnick (1990). Torgovnick

(1990: 143–45), for instance, notes that *Heart of Darkness* both reiterates primitivist tropes and critiques imperialism. In *Heart of Darkness* Marlow recounts to a group of sailors the story of his journey into the African interior toward Kurtz's "Inner Station," a brutal, ivory-trading camp. The following excerpt from Marlow's narrative offers a taste of the primitivist tropes that establish Africa as a dark, "primitive," and impenetrable site:

> We penetrated deeper and deeper into the heart of darkness.... We were wanderers on a prehistoric earth, on an earth that wore the aspect of an unknown planet. We could have fancied ourselves the first men taking possession of an accursed inheritance, to be subdued at the cost of profound anguish and excessive toil. But suddenly, as we struggled round a bend, there would be a glimpse of rush walls, of peaked grass roofs, a burst of yells, a whirl of black limbs, a mass of hands clapping, of feet stamping, of bodies swaying, of eyes rolling, under the droop of heavy and motionless foliage. The steamer toiled along slowly on the edge of a black and incomprehensible frenzy. The prehistoric man was cursing us, praying to us, welcoming us—who could tell? We were cut off from the comprehension of our surroundings; we glided past like phantoms, wondering and secretly appalled, as sane men would do before an enthusiastic outbreak in a madhouse. We could not remember because we were traveling in the night of the first ages, of those ages that are gone, leaving hardly a sign—and no memories. (Conrad 1982: 50–51)

But aside from reiterating primitivist tropes, Conrad also criticizes Belgian colonialism and the European will to power with his thinly veiled reference to King Leopold II's reign of terror over the Congo Free State at the end of the nineteenth century. Marlow describes colonial domination with ambivalence: "The conquest of the earth, which mostly means the taking it away from those who have a different complexion or slightly flatter noses than ourselves, is not a pretty thing when you look into it too much. What redeems it is the idea only" (Conrad 1982: 10). Indeed, Marlow is captivated by "the idea" of colonialism. He describes Kurtz's report for the "International Society for the Suppression of Savage Customs" as "eloquent," "altruistic," and "noble." But at the end of the report Kurtz has scrawled the horrifying words, "Exterminate all the brutes!" Describing Kurtz, Marlow says: "Everything belonged to him—but that was a trifle. The thing was to know what he belonged to, how many powers of darkness claimed him for their own" (Conrad 1982: 70–72). Thus, Kurtz's descent into greed and terror takes place in its own realm of darkness, for which Africa is a metaphor. The resulting ideological ambivalence of *Heart of Darkness* is evoked by Miller: "It is neither colonialistic enough to be damnable nor ironic enough to be completely untainted by 'colonialistic bias.' The net effect is a subversion of Africanist discourse from within" (1985: 171).

Cannizzo clearly worked with a similarly nuanced understanding of *Heart of Darkness*. As she explains in her post-mortem review of *Into the Heart of Africa*, the exhibit title was intended to echo Conrad's *Heart of Darkness*, "which dealt not only with the alleged darkness of the 'Dark Continent' but most clearly with the 'darkness' within the colonists themselves" (Cannizzo 1991a: 151). Thus, Cannizzo wanted to stress *Heart of Darkness* as an evocation of psychological and cultural crisis.[7] But as we have seen, visitors to the exhibit did not always understand this ambiguity. *Heart of Darkness* is lumped together with various missionary and explorer pronouncements about the "dark continent," even though the spirit of Conrad's narrative is different than that of his contemporaries. Explaining the complex intertextuality that shapes Africanist discourse, Miller writes:

> Millennia before Conrad's "unreadable report" in Heart of Darkness, a tradition without a beginning had been established and perpetuated. Texts on Africa were severely limited in number until the nineteenth century and tended to repeat each other in a sort of cannibalistic, plagiarizing intertextuality. Pliny repeats Herodotus, who repeats Homer, just as later French and English writers will copy each other and even copy the Ancients. (1985: 6)

Cannizzo is working within (and against) this tradition, so that her language cannot be separated from a larger legacy of writing about Africa that includes Conrad, the explorer H.M. Stanley who wrote *Through the Dark Continent* (1878) and *Through Darkest Africa* (1890), and Georg Schweinfurth, the German botanist and author of a popular travel book entitled *The Heart of Africa* (1874).

Democratizing Museums

In fact, many members of the CFTA did understand and appreciate Cannizzo's critical intentions. However, an intellectual understanding of *Into the Heart of Africa* did not diminish the hurt they experienced in viewing the exhibit. One protestor noted that while he could decipher the exhibit's irony, he still felt "the emotion of the rape of I and I." Similarly, a local curator, who was marginally associated with the CFTA, stated that she found the exhibit to be both successful and "visually horrifying." Given their own emotional reactions to *Into the Heart of Africa*, these people were most often concerned about the potential impact of the exhibit upon visitors who might not read its irony. Thus, CFTA members and other critics often suggested that *Into the Heart of Africa* was a "curators' exhibit" or, that it was only appropriate for people with a university education (Lyons and Lyons n.d.: 15–16). In contextualizing their critiques of *Into the Heart of Africa* in this way, these critics underlined the ROM's history of elitism.

Museums, however, are under pressure to broaden their notions of the public, and to thus play a role in democratizing knowledge. Influenced by these ideals, critics of *Into the Heart of Africa* often made a distinction between academic interests and public responsibilities.[8] This distinction was vividly illustrated to me when I interviewed a member of the CFTA who was reading *On Revelation and Revolution: Christianity, Colonialism, and Consciousness in South Africa* (1991) by Jean and John Comaroff. I noted a strong contrast between this woman's academic interest in *On Revelation and Revolution*—an historical ethnography that re-presents imperial images and discourses similar to those employed by Cannizzo—and her concerns about *Into the Heart of Africa*. Her concerns focused on children's potential mis-readings of the exhibit:

> If museums are supposed to be educational institutions, then it didn't work at all. Because one is thinking that young children and older children will be coming to this exhibition, and young children especially do not have the intellectual tools to grasp, you know, these ironies. And surely, adolescents, unless they have been given a lot of thought to certain things, also cannot grasp these ironies.

She imagined how a child might experience the Military Hall:

> People are more influenced by visual images, you know. So when you enter the museum and you see Lord Beresford piercing the heart of a Zulu soldier, and then beside it another picture of Zulu soldiers and these soldiers are described as wild savages, or something like that—that's what frustrated me. And in the same chamber you see a map titled "Darkest Africa," in quotes of course. Well I'd say that when a ten-year-old child goes into that chamber and sees "Darkest Africa"—it's supposed to be ironic, you know because it's in quotes—but it doesn't work, it has failed. Because what that does, all these images and pictures and maps, is just to reinforce in people the old stereotype of Africa the wild, savage place.

Such concerns about the potential negative impact of *Into the Heart of Africa* upon children were heightened by the fact that some classes had negative experiences while visiting the exhibit. Janet McClelland, a teacher at Essex Public School, visited *Into the Heart of Africa* twice, and during each visit she found that tour guides uncritically reiterated the exhibit's primitivist discourses. On McClelland's first visit to the exhibit in December 1989, a guide said that "the missionaries civilized the pagans of Africa" and that the Zulu were "an extremely vicious tribe" (McClelland 1990: 10). When McClelland visited the exhibit in February 1990 with her grade 5 and 6 class, a guide explained: "Here we see carpentry that Africans learned from missionaries," and "Here we see a spoon carved of wood. Missionaries taught the Africans to carve wood." Challenged on this point, the guide explained that

Africans did carve art, but did not create useful objects until contact with missionaries. Another guide stated that a mask was used to practice "barbaric rituals, vicious, barbaric rituals" (apparently the guide was referring to female circumcision). And another guide said to the students: "See how the African girls put pieces of ivory through their noses. Think how that would hurt. Weren't they crazy to do that." Given this irruption of primitivist tropes, it is not surprising that one student remarked that "it seemed to him that the Africans didn't have a thought of their own." In fact this is not an isolated incident. In *Primitive Art in Civilized Places*, Sally Price recounts a similar museum guide incident (1989). While visiting the Michael C. Rockefeller wing of the Metropolitan Museum of Art in New York in 1984, a security guard gave Price an informal, unsolicited lecture about "the primitive," which focused on such exotic themes as cannibalism, voodoo, and female circumcision. Both Price and Marianna Torgovnick (1990) remind us of the theoretical point that such notions of "the primitive" are not completely uninformed, but are always exaggerated, distorted, and decontextualized. As Hari Lalla noted with regard to the ROM guides: "The guides were ill-trained and often offered racist interpretations. This was not intentional; they were just adding their little understandings."

This matter was of grave concern to the Toronto Board of Education, since many school groups would be visiting *Into the Heart of Africa*. In May 1990, an assessment of the exhibit was prepared for the Toronto Board of Education by Hari Lalla, who was Curriculum Advisor in Race Relations and Multiculturalism, and John Myers, a History and Contemporary Studies Consultant. Lalla and Myers concluded that *Into the Heart of Africa* had no direct educational value for elementary school students, and that if secondary school classes viewed the exhibit they should be given both extensive preparatory and follow-up activities. The authors suggested that "a more effective exhibition could have juxtaposed additional exhibitions, charts, maps, short videos and commentary under the theme *The truth about the peoples of Africa during this period of exploitation*" (Lalla and Myers 1990: 4). In light of this report, the Toronto Board of Education recommended that the school groups consult with the CFTA before planning to visit *Into the Heart of Africa*. This recommendation is significant since it reflects a tension between the Toronto Board of Education and the ROM, two institutions that play a central role in socializing children and re-producing society. In contrast with the ROM, the Toronto Board of Education perceived the CFTA as a legitimate organization that could contextualize *Into the Heart of Africa* for school children.[9] In this way, black children would not risk experiencing the sense of dehumanization evoked by lawyer and CFTA member Charles Roach: "I look around but can find little about Africans. Their biographies are not here. Unlike the soldiers and missionaries they are devoid of personality. Canadian missionaries and soldiers are described as the 'Cultural Self': Africans as the 'Ethnographic Other'" (1990: A17).

Ironically, Cannizzo was aware of this issue of objectification, on a theoretical level. In an essay entitled "How Sweet It Is: Cultural Politics in
Barbados," she critiques the political inequities of the Barbados National
Museum which, until recently, focused uniquely on exhibiting the stories of
plantation owners and their families: "By not displaying the cultural heritage
of the majority of the population, the museum has taken from them, by implication, their role as history makers, as active participants in their own
history" (1987: 24). Yet, as we have seen, Cannizzo did not engage with
members of the black community as active history makers. Nor did she
explore how members of the black community relate to the ROM's African
collection today, as they seek to define themselves within the Canadian state.
Finally, Roach's comment suggests that *Into the Heart of Africa* did not disrupt the traditional "subject/object relationship" (hooks 1990: 143) that has
characterized anthropology and museums. Julie Cruikshank situates this issue
in a larger theoretical and political context:

> Museums and anthropology are undeniably part of a western philosophical tradi-
> tion, embedded in a dualism which becomes problematic as a conceptual frame-
> work for addressing issues of representation. Entrenched oppositions between
> 'self/other', 'subject/object', 'us/them', inevitably leave power in the hands of
> the defining institution. (1992: 6)

Given this theoretical legacy, it is not surprising that minority groups often
define the very act of speaking as politically empowering, for speaking "constitutes a subject that challenges and subverts the opposition between the
knowing agent and the object of knowledge" (Alcoff 1991: 23). In this sense,
the CFTA pamphlet can be read as an interruption of the traditional
subject/object opposition that informs exhibits. Stephen Inglis suggests that
the pamphlet produced by the CFTA may represent "a new genre in 'museum'
publication" (1990: 103). Certainly, the CFTA succeeded in extending the text
of *Into the Heart of Africa* beyond the walls of the museum (Philip 1991).

A Counter-Text: The CFTA Pamphlet

The CFTA pamphlet "The Truth About Africa" made only a few direct references to *Into the Heart of Africa* (see Appendix 1). Instead, the six-page pamphlet presented a list of "Africa's contributions to humanity" in areas of
knowledge such as medicine, art, science, astronomy, architecture, mathematics, religion, and steel making. The first three entries in this list of achievements were as follows:

Creators of Medicine
"During the millennia, blacks in ancient Egypt made numerous contributions to
medicine and were acknowledged as the inventors of the art of medicine. They

produced the earliest physicians, medical knowledge, and medical literature. They contributed to the development of medicine in ancient Greece. Ancient writers affirm this."

Frederick Newsome M.D.
Journal of African Contributions

Creators of Art
"The first artist was Black. The oldest sculpture in the world, the 'Bas-Relief of White Rhinoceros with Ticks' was found in South Africa."

J. A. Rogers, Sex and Race Vol.1

Creators of Science
"Socrates (a black African), in the Phaidros, called the Egyptian god Thoth, the inventor of writing, astronomy, and geometry. Herodotus had a similarly high opinion of Egyptian science, stating that Greeks learned geometry from the Egyptians."

Dr. John Papperdemos, Professor of Physics,
University of Illinois

The CFTA's concern with African origins and achievements, and with what they regard as "black" Egypt is evident in these excerpts. This distinct orientation towards reconstructing African history is represented in the academy by Afrocentric scholars such as Cheikh Anta Diop who worked with the Institut Fondmental de l'Afrique Noire (IFAN) in Dakar, and Molefi Kete Asante, chairman of the African-American Studies department at Temple University. It is worth noting the extent to which the CFTA pamphlet echoed the work of both Diop and Asante.

Among Diop's numerous publications is *The African Origin of Civilization* where he claims that:

> The ancient Egyptians were Negroes. The moral fruit of their civilization is to be counted among the assets of the Black world. Instead of presenting itself to history as an insolvent debtor, that Black world is the very initiator of the "western" civilization flaunted before our eyes today. (1974: xiv)

To develop this thesis, Diop suggests that Egyptians recognized their ancestors as coming from Nubia and from "the heart of Africa" (1974: 150). Asante, in his numerous works, explores similar lines of thought to Diop. For instance, in *The Afrocentric Idea* he states:

> From Africa, the seat of the oldest organized civilizations as well as the birthplace of humanity, rhetorical models and interest traveled across the sea to Sicily, Greece, and Rome. The rise of Egypt and Nubia, its mother, is conservatively put at 5000 years before the rise of Greek civilization. Greek students had

studied in Africa even prior to the matriculation of Socrates and Plato at the temples. (1987: 166)

Rico was passionate about this subject:

> Knowledge of navigation by the stars and by the sun came directly from Kemet. Kemet is known as Egypt through the Greek.... Kemet then got its knowledge from the HEART of Africa. This is the irony of the whole thing. Where is the heart of Africa? Follow the Nile to its sources, there is the heart of Africa. Places that is called Uganda, places that is called Ethiopia. Egypt has some of the most, what do you call it, sources of the Nile. So I'm telling you that the Greeks learned mathematics... astrology, astronomy and all those things from Kemet. Kemet learned it from deeper in Africa. Knowledge does not flow up-river. It flows down-river.

In fact, this continuity of thought played itself out in a very concrete way during the ROM controversy. Asante, who dedicates *The Afrocentric Idea* to Diop and to W. E. B. DuBois, was invited by the CFTA to come to Toronto to view *Into the Heart of Africa*.

On July 12, 1990, Asante viewed *Into the Heart of Africa* and then addressed a meeting of the CFTA. Not surprisingly, Asante (1990: 63) critiqued the exhibit, stating that it "reinforced that same kind of arrogance the missionaries had" and that such a fragmentary presentation of Africa "gives a very, very negative impression." He stated:

> When I saw this exhibit, I thought, it is worthy of Alabama in the 1950s or South Africa today, but not Toronto at present. It is not Into the Heart of Africa, because it does not understand Africa. Whether you take archeological or biological evidence... there's no genre of knowledge that you cannot trace back to the continent of Africa. (1990: 63)

How, Asante asked, could the ROM minimize African achievements while emphasizing minor white ones? Following this theme, the CFTA pamphlet stated that the theme of *Into the Heart of Africa* should be changed, or else the exhibit be closed.

The logic of this argument is very similar to that made by Chinua Achebe with regard to Conrad's *Heart of Darkness*. In his controversial essay entitled "An Image of Africa" (1977), Achebe argues that *Heart of Darkness* is racist, and should not be taught. Achebe critiques Conrad for making the story of two European men of greater importance than the entire continent. Resisting this Eurocentric narrative structure, Achebe states that he looks forward to the day when "Western man may begin to look seriously at the achievements of other people" (1977: 793).

The approach to African history proposed by the CFTA is very different from that of critics such as Torgovnick (1990) and Edward Said (1993a), who favour teaching Conrad in order to examine imperialist ideology and

Conrad's complex relationship to it. Like Torgovnick and Said, I favour "teaching the conflicts" (Graff 1992), which means teaching colonial and imperial history. As Said (1993b) has said: "It's not what you read, it's how you read it." In contrast, the CFTA appeared to dismiss this relational approach to history: "Our difficulty with the ROM is not with their carrying an African exhibit, but with the remarks accompanying these paintings, carvings, photos, etc. This exhibit thus reminds us too vividly of a past that is still not past" (CFTA 1990: 5). This response to *Into the Heart of Africa* was also articulated by journalist Robert Payne:

> Canada's most racially and culturally mixed city deserves better than a show sure to rip open old wounds. Is this the best use of taxpayers' money? What next, an exhibit of Nazi photographs and relics of the Holocaust? Many of our recent immigrants have marched to the beat of the colonial drummer. Few lament its demise. There was little demand to resurrect its memory, except perhaps among longtime Canadians who miss the good old days of raping and pillaging foreign cultures. (1990: 64)

Here, Payne expresses a desire to distance himself from a traumatic past. Such a desire is not uncommon. In *The Past is a Foreign Country*, David Lowenthal notes that "people often strive to forget or banish a baneful inheritance" (1985: 66). On the other hand, the recovery of memory and stories often enables people to live with experiences of loss or discontinuity (see, for example, Myerhoff 1986, 1987).

Significantly, one member of the CFTA whom I interviewed distanced himself from Payne's remark. This was my first sense of the fluid nature of the CFTA discourse, despite its apparent essentialism. During our discussions (which were certainly shaped by the fact that the ROM controversy was now past), CFTA members offered more nuanced opinions than were represented in their pamphlet. They also contextualized their resistance to *Into the Heart of Africa*. For instance, one woman said that the primary problem with *Into the Heart of Africa* was not its relational approach to history per se, but rather its lack of explicit statement about the costs of colonialism:

> They didn't tell the story of Africa. And it's really sad because I think history was distorted. To me that was a period when Africa faced the most vicious form of colonialism. Africans were dispossessed. It [the exhibit] was a denial of the process. One had glimpses of it. But it was like they were trying to pretty up, to give a vicious thing a pretty face. And they did.[10]

Another CFTA member was especially concerned about the euphemistic nature of the word "collect":

> Is collected a euphemism for raping and ravishing—a lot of these things were stolen you know. And after the conquest of Benin, soldiers just went in

and looted. And that's why museums got their exhibits. From pillaging and plundering.

This critique is very much like the one made by Alfonzo Ortiz when he spoke about the Columbian Quincentenary at the American Anthropological Meetings in Chicago in 1991. Ortiz found anthropological interest in colonial "encounters" to be rather euphemistic and detached.

Finally, members of the CFTA and other critics appeared to have ambivalent feelings about exhibiting colonial history. Hesitations about teaching colonial history were difficult to separate from concerns about the detached nature of irony. As Tara Chadwick, the anthropology student said: "I'm not sure whether I would even have written the text in that way. It's sort of calling up memories of those words. I think its sort of like hitting someone on a bruise. It's just too awful a memory, and too intense emotions to deal with again." This comment suggests that subject-positions and irony are profoundly connected. I will return to this observation in my afterword, when I discuss the possibilities of reflexive curatorship.

Contradictions of Resistance

It is important to evaluate the "ideological atmosphere" (Mudimbe 1988: 99) of the CFTA discourse. In general terms, the CFTA discourse is an example of Afrocentrism, which draws from a long black nationalist tradition (West 1992). Diop's work, for example, is informed by intellectual and political nationalism. He responds to the "classical theme 'all that is European is civilized; all that is African is barbarous,' with the declaration that 'all that is African is civilized and beautiful'" (Mudimbe 1988: 169). Edward Said (1992: 178–9) notes that the negritude movement that invigorated decolonization struggles in French Africa also depended upon such reversals. While the epistemology of imperialism marked "natives" as inferior "others," the negritude movement revalorized and celebrated alterity. Said understands the negritude movement as representing a particular historical moment when blacks sought to reclaim and remake their history and identity.

However, scholars such as Mudimbe, West, and Said do not hesitate to critique the ways in which Afrocentrism mimics the logic of Eurocentrism. This paradox is especially relevant to any consideration of the CFTA discourse. Michael Lambek alluded to this aspect of mimicry in the CFTA discourse:

Some of the critics [of *Into the Heart of Africa*] seemed to feel that African culture will only be of value when it is made to take on the achievements of the "master narratives" of European history. But to want to make over African culture and history is misguided. It is to succumb to the very colonialist mentality which we want to escape. (1990: 2)

In my interviews, I asked members of the CFTA and other critics of *Into the Heart of Africa* to respond to this critique of the CFTA's discourse. People tended to view Lambek's point about mimicry as an interesting theoretical issue, but far less important than the need to research and re-present new histories about Africa and Africans. Hari Lalla, for example, viewed the exhibit's self-reflexive tone as "a luxury" given the fact that "we have so little information about Africa." Similarly, David Sutherland, a student of anthropology and film at York University, stated that re-presenting black history is "a matter of first principles." He went on to describe a formative event in his own life when a past white "friend" said to him: "You people didn't do anything. Your people are on welfare. We created the welfare system. We have Renoir. We have Rembrandt." It was in this context that Sutherland spoke about the importance of learning about black history and the lack of opportunity to do so in schools and museums in Canada.

CFTA members tended to raise concerns about reclaiming history in particularly self-aggrandizing terms. For instance, Rico stated: "If you are going to do destructive things about I, you may as well put some historical accuracy to it. You cannot call I backward when I and I showed the I how to sail." In Diop's language, such recognition of Africa's contributions represents "the plain unvarnished truth" (Diop 1974: 235). Because Afrocentrists tend to pose as keepers of an imagined essential truth, many scholars, journalists, and educators (and I include myself here) react with skepticism. Cornel West notes that Afrocentrists such as Asante (and the more extreme Leonard Jeffries) lack a

> subtle enough sense of history, so they can't recognize ambiguous legacies of traditions and civilizations. They refuse to recognize the thoroughly hybrid culture of almost every culture we have ever discovered. In the case of Jeffries, this lack of subtlety slides down an ugly xenophobic slope—a mirror image of the Eurocentric racism he condemns. (1992: 237–8)

Educators have noted that Afrocentric curriculums risk falling into facile "ethnic boosterism" (Ravitch 1992: 285) and reductive notions of identity (Gates 1992a). Given the prevailing skepticism about Afrocentrism in the United States, it is quite surprising that the Toronto Board of Education endorsed the CFTA. It appears that Canadian cultural and educational politics do not necessarily follow American patterns, despite common assumptions otherwise.

Henry Louis Gates suggests ways in which we can analyze the tensions inherent in Afrocentric discourses. He makes a distinction between theoretical concerns about epistemology and a need to respond to everyday conditions of racial domination that people experience. Gates describes this contradiction as a tension between the "imperatives of agency" and the "rhetoric of dismantlement" (1991: 34). This ideological tension influenced Gates' efforts to edit an Afro-American anthology. Gates describes how critics on the left are suspicious of his efforts to create an Afro-American canon; these critics argue that any canon is "hierarchical, patriarchal, and otherwise politically suspect" (1991: 31). However, in response to this epistemological critique, Gates defends his efforts to create a new Afro-American canon, arguing that people previously marginalized and silenced must have an opportunity to discover other representations of themselves.

It was with regard to this idea of the imperatives of agency that most protestors (and other people I interviewed) explained the meaning of the name "Coalition for the Truth about Africa." CFTA members described their call for "the truth about Africa" as a reaction to Western stereotypes of Africa, which they felt *Into the Heart of Africa* reiterated. As a member of the CFTA explained to me: "People felt that it [the exhibit] wasn't the truth. You know, because they say we're going to take you on a historical tour of Africa. So the coalition felt that it should set itself up as a body to divulge a part of the truth or some of the truth." Here, truth is defined in opposition to the ROM's status as truth-teller. Considering that the CFTA suspected the ROM of endorsing missionary discourses, it is interesting to note that missionary speech also calls on "the authority of the truth" (Mudimbe 1988: 47). As Mudimbe explains, "the missionary does not enter into dialogue with pagans and "savages" but must impose the law of God that he incarnates" (1988: 47). This presents an interesting parallel with the CFTA's claim to know "the truth" about Africa. The CFTA discourse is certainly not original in its claim to truth. It seems to reiterate the logic of missionary discourse, but whereas the missionary discourse is driven by absolutes—the secure knowledge that missionaries have a duty to save Africa—some members of the CFTA spoke about "the truth" in a more contingent and relational fashion than their pamphlet suggested.

A similar contingent use of the word "truth" is found in Dawson Munjeri's remarks concerning the historical complicity between museums and colonial domination in Zimbabwe. Colonial museums excelled in documenting accounts of colonial achievements and presented blacks as "primitive," voiceless, relics. Black students were discouraged from visiting museums, and until the 1950s, blacks were not included in visitor statistics. In reaction to the injustice of such exclusion (both symbolic and material), Munjeri writes: "There should have been an emphasis on the truth about the country and all its peoples. Part of that truth was that the country was multiracial and its cultural wealth lay in the diversity of its cultures" (1991: 454). Another example of the highly relational nature of some truth claims is found in Kristi Evans' research on underground Solidarity stamps in Poland. These unofficial stamps re-presented Polish history and national identity in ways not recognized by the Communist state. Thus, these stamps circulated as forms of symbolic resistance, demonstrating Solidarity's "claim to the possession of truth, especially the objectively 'true' history of Poland" (Evans 1992: 749). Evans notes that Solidarity's notion of truth had many connotations. The labor union's iconography expressed itself in opposition to the Communist state, commemorating events that "really happened," as well as notions of religious truth that Communism denied (Evans 1992: 763).

While members of the CFTA stressed the relational nature of their rhetoric, its essentialist expressions cannot be ignored. As Rico once said to me:

> There is only one truth about Africa. Existentially there's only one truth. However there is a partitioning of those truths culturally, but there's only one truth about Africa. And the only people who can tell that truth about Africa is African peoples.

Here, Rico asserts a fixed, essential notion of identity. This assertion raises difficult issues about the relationship between knowledge and experience. "True knowledge" is equated with the experience of being black. The ideological atmosphere of this statement is complex, since it claims the right to self-representation while simultaneously reiterating European categories of race and notions of racial purity. In identifying this tension within the CFTA discourse, I am influenced by Mudimbe's nuanced analysis of the life and work of Edward Blyden. It is useful to briefly refer to Blyden, as his work is an important historical touchstone for any consideration of themes of black identity and resistance.

Blyden was born in the West Indies in 1832. He emigrated to West Africa in 1851. In Africa, he wrote numerous works, such as *Vindication of the Negro Race* (1857), *Liberia's Offering* (1862), *The Negro in Ancient History* (1869), and *Christianity, Islam and the Negro Race* (1857). He developed a unique position on colonization, advocating that Africa should be colonized by "civilized blacks from America" (in Mudimbe 1988: 104). He also believed that by emigrating to Africa, black Americans could attain "true manhood" (in Mudimbe 1988: 104).

Mudimbe offers two different ways of interpreting Blyden's work. On the one hand, Blyden's writing can be read as a reaction to European practices of denigrating Africans. Like the CFTA, Blyden emphasized the need for Africans and people of African descent to reclaim their history. Blyden urged Africans to re-interpret the history of their continent, "about which the truth is yet to be found out" (in Mudimbe 1988: 122). This is the empowering message in Blyden's work. However, Mudimbe also points out that Blyden vigorously employed notions of racial difference and racial purity that informed the most suspect nineteenth-century theories of racial inequality. A similar tension between self-determination and racial determinism exists in the CFTA discourse.[11]

Claims of authority based on the color of one's skin are, as Gayatri Spivak (1989) and Edward Said (1993a) have argued, deterministic and exclusionary. Spivak calls such ideological moves "chromatism" (1989: 62). Chromatism, for example, allows privileged whites to avoid histories of imperialism. Spivak recounts the case of a white undergraduate male who earnestly stated: "I am only a bourgeois white male, I can't speak" (in Spivak 1989: 62). Spivak's opinion of such matters is similar to that of writer Jamaica Kincaid, who contributes an important forward to Guy Endore's novel *Babouk* (originally published in 1934). *Babouk* is a story about slavery that is loosely based on the Haitian slave insurrection of 1791. Kincaid writes that Endore (who died in 1970) was

> a white man and he wrote a work of fiction, a passionate account of the life of an African slave.... I am glad that the author of this book was a white person. I think that every white writer should write a book about black slavery, as I think every writer who is not a Jew should write a book about the Holocaust. (Kincaid 1991: viii)

Here, Kincaid appreciates the pedagogical and moral power of crossing boundaries and of seeking "imaginative identification" (Rorty 1989: 93) with others.

In contrast, the CFTA tended to define authority and voice in rigid terms, although their rhetoric was not without moments of humour and openings for negotiation and discussion. Once, when I asked a member of the CFTA if he would work with a white anthropologist, he replied: "I'm sitting here talking with you, aren't I?" Another CFTA member I interviewed never expressed essentialist notions about race and ethnographic authority. Rather, she raised questions concerning inequitable access to resources and opportunities to carry out research. She wondered, for example, why indigenous people rarely have the opportunity to study their own culture. Moreover, she hoped simply that scholars such as Cannizzo would be more sensitive to, and aware of, these sorts of power relations.

Members of the black community who did not identify with the CFTA were often critical of the group's reductive notions of identity. Frustrated by strict boundaries of gender and race, Sutherland said:

> Well the boundaries, of course you know, they're man made. These days more and more people are talking about these things ... who can speak for who, and if your experience isn't exactly like mine, like if I didn't grow up in metro housing, you know, you ain't really black you know. Or if you didn't grow up in Jane

Finch or whatever, you're not down because you didn't understand exactly what I went through. And everybody's positioning themselves as the ultimate victim.

Tara Chadwick expressed a similar frustration with the politics of representation according to the CFTA: "I have a big thing about the designation of races. Partly because of my non-designation! I think that they [the CFTA] were perpetuating the dichotomy between European and non-European. That bothered me." Interestingly, despite their reservations about the CFTA, both Sutherland and Chadwick thought that the coalition played a useful role in creating awareness about racism in Toronto. Here, we turn to the subject of performance and spectacle.

Racism and Multiculturalism: Articulating a Contradiction

Once the protestors clashed with the police, the CFTA increasingly used *Into the Heart of Africa*—an exhibit about the past—as a way of speaking about contemporary racism in Canadian society. For instance, Charles Roach, who is a prominent member of the Black Action Defense Committee, regarded the exhibit as

> offensive in that it glorified acts like the slaying of Zulus, which really was the precursor to apartheid and the enslavement of Africans in their own country. I said that the photograph of the soldier plunging his sword into the African's heart is pretty chilling in light of the police shootings of [Lester] Donaldson and [Sophia] Cook in Toronto. (in Nazareth 1990: 11)

Roach's particular use of *Into the Heart of Africa* illustrates the way in which artifacts exist "simultaneously in the past and present" (Lowenthal 1985: 248).

The ROM controversy cannot be isolated from larger political contexts, particularly policing issues in Toronto. On May 14, 1990—nine days after CFTA members first clashed with police at the ROM—Marlon Neal was shot by the Metro police. Two weeks later, on June 2, 1990, Hanzel Alonzo died in police custody (he had been arrested on May 18, 1990). On the day of Alonzo's death, protestors again clashed with the police, and nine members of the CFTA were arrested on various counts including obstructing and assaulting the police, escaping lawful custody, and assault with the intent to resist arrest. The confrontation was triggered when police attempted to arrest CFTA member Oji Adisa, who was wanted on an arrest warrant that related to the first clash between the CFTA and the police.

As these events occurred, the CFTA increasingly linked symbolic and political domination. As Roach stated to the *Toronto Sun* on June 10, 1990: "The struggles with the ROM and the Metro Police are welded together.

Inside the ROM is institutional racism and outside is the brutal reality." Demonstrating this point of solidarity, the CFTA joined a crowd of some 500 people who were protesting the shooting of Marlon Neal outside police headquarters on June 10, 1990. Another indicator of the hybridism of these issues is reflected by the fact that on May 23, 1990, leaders of the black community—including members of the CFTA—met with then Premier David Peterson to discuss police shootings, racism, and *Into the Heart of Africa*. A similar fusing of issues is evoked by Dionne Brand in her poem entitled "Out There," which begins:

> In this country only nailed in the air with words, the heart of darkness is these white roads, snow at our throats, and at the windshield a thick white cop in a blue steel windbreaker peering into our car suspiciously, even in the blow and freeze of a snowstorm, or, perhaps not suspicion, but as a man looking at aliens. Three Blacks in a car
> On a road blowing eighty miles an hour in the wind between a gas station and Chatham. We stumble on our antiquity. The snow blue laser of a cop's eyes fixes us in this unbearable archeology.

> (1992: 155)

Here, Brand has turned the phrase "heart of darkness" in on itself, so that it is made to signify her own experience of "otherness" in Canada. Clearly, colonialism's "violence of the gaze" (Alloula 1986: 31) is both historical and contemporary.[12]

A significant and evocative alliance was formed on July 15, 1990 when the CFTA was joined by natives protesting the confrontations between police and Mohawks in Oka, Quebec. The allied groups marched from the ROM to the downtown Eaton Center, which houses Quebec government offices.[13] Lennox Farrell of the Black Action Defense Committee stated, "The black community stands behind the Mohawk people in their demands in Oka and other places."[14] John Brooks of the Akwesasne Warrior Society quoted Malcolm X by wearing a t-shirt that said: "By any means necessary." This brief alliance between natives and blacks reveals the pragmatic, shifting nature of alliances of resistance in popular culture. As John Fiske writes in *Understanding Popular Culture*:

> The necessity of negotiating the problems of everyday life within a complex, highly elaborated social structure has produced nomadic subjectivities who can move around ... realigning their social allegiances into different formations of the people according to the necessities of the moment. All these reformulations are made within a structure of power relations, all social allegiances have not only a sense of *with whom*, but also of *against whom*. (1989: 24)

Indeed, when blacks and natives came together in protest, they shared a goal of demonstrating against racism and domination in general, and against police racism and violence in particular. They voiced these complaints together, speaking as visible minorities in the Canadian mosaic.

The demonstrations at the ROM deeply challenged Canada's official policy of multiculturalism, which valorizes harmonious cultural diversity. A kit for teachers prepared by the ROM offers a good example of this idea of ethnic harmony. The kit explained that upon viewing *Into the Heart of Africa* "we are confronted with a turn of the century world view very different from that which now exists in the multicultural reality of Canadian school classrooms."[15] Here, the ROM's statement reflects a liberal understanding of multiculturalism that seeks to "affirm difference within a politics of consensus" (Giroux 1992: 14). In contrast, the CFTA asserted that racism and political struggle are central to the experience of difference in Canada. In making this point, the CFTA shared concerns with post-colonial critic Homi Bhabha (1990) who analyzes the paradox of why countries with policies that endorse and accommodate cultural diversity still experience racism. This occurs, Bhabha explains, because "the universalism that paradoxically permits diversity masks ethnocentric norms, values and interests" (1990: 208). Thus, the CFTA made it known that Toronto is not all harmonious ethnic kiosks and innocent cultural sharing. And in exposing this "truth" about Toronto, the crisis at the ROM extended far beyond *Into the Heart of Africa*. Ironically, *Into the Heart of Africa* was partially funded by the Ontario Ministry for Multiculturalism.

Chapter V

Various Positions: Responses to the Coalition for the Truth about Africa

Beyond *Into the Heart of Africa*

The debates around *Into the Heart of Africa* extended far beyond the exhibit itself. Most people involved in, or touched by the controversy, positioned themselves in complex ways in relation to the exhibit, Cannizzo, and the CFTA. Consequently, many people I interviewed expressed differently nuanced evaluations of the controversy, rarely situating themselves squarely on one side of the debate. However, fluidity was not apparent in dominant constructions of the controversy. The ROM, the media, and the CFTA, contributed to creating a highly polarized "us versus them" debate. This chapter begins by examining how the ROM and the media marginalized and radicalized the CFTA. Following this, I will consider the more complex responses of academics and members of the black community to the CFTA. As will become clear, people in these communities approached the controversy with a sense of multiplicity and awareness of competing ideologies and political priorities. In a larger sense, the CFTA was a catalyst for discussion and reflection about minority rights, resistance, complicity, and academic freedom. Finally, I will consider alternative voices from within the ROM—staff members who distanced themselves from the ROM's "official" discourse, and identified museological issues raised by the controversy. In this way, the richness of the ROM controversy can be better appreciated.

Authority at/of the ROM

As we have seen, the atmosphere of the ROM controversy was one of extreme polarization. On the one hand, protestors demanded that *Into the*

Heart of Africa be closed down as a condition for further discussions. And on the other hand, on May 16, 1990, the ROM succeeded in having the Supreme Court of Ontario issue an injunction that restricted the CFTA from picketing within 50 feet of the museum entrance. As positions became entrenched, the CFTA and the ROM both continued to speak, but not directly to each other. The CFTA communicated its position in the media in its pamphlets, and simply by making its presence known outside the museum. By standing in the shadow of the monumental museum, the CFTA enacted their concerns about being excluded from public culture in general, and the exhibiting process in particular.

The ROM communicated its position to the media through its Marketing and Public Information Department. Ironically, the Marketing and Public Information Department—which is meant to facilitate communication between the museum and the public—added to many critics' perceptions of the ROM as being a bureaucratic, impenetrable fortress. This feeling is apparent, for example, in a video of the protests made by David Sutherland, Azed Majeed, and Firoza Elavia. The six minute video juxtaposes voices of protestors ("Your local museum is armed and dangerous. Watch out.") with voices of ROM staff. A number of times during the video a phone rings and an impersonal voice answers, "Linda Thomas, Public Relations at the ROM." The words "THEFT" and "AUTHORITY" flash on the screen when a ROM voice says: "The ROM is a big museum. We have procedures that we go through. Well I just can't let you in right now. You can call me back Monday." In fact, the video makers did go into the museum with their camera, where they got a shaky shot of the Lord Beresford engraving before being requested by a security guard to stop filming. Sutherland explained to me that the video team knew that they would not succeed in filming the exhibit, but that they wanted to capture on film the effect of being "shut down." For Sutherland, this aspect of the video was a way of expressing his frustration with the "whole bureaucracy of the thing and how it's pushed against you. They've got all their speeches prepared. They've got the proper mechanisms to frustrate you. You know, any bureaucracy just wants to keep itself alive." Like Sutherland, Stephen Weil (1990) is not optimistic about the ability of large, bureaucratic museums to respond imaginatively to local community concerns. Like any other bureaucratic organization, internal communication in large museums is impersonal and is structured by hierarchical relations. Problem-solving is guided by rules and procedures. This alienates ad hoc community groups, such as the CFTA, which form around a sense of common values, solidarity, and direct action (Rothschild and Whitt 1986). For Sutherland, the ROM's organizational atmosphere distracts from its higher purpose of creating "brilliant works" and "engaging exhibits."

For large museums such as the ROM, managing and protecting the collections is a central concern. When the ROM issued its injunction against the

CFTA, it noted that the museum "has an obligation under the Royal Ontario Museum Act of 1968 to protect its collections, visitors and staff from any threat to safety."[1] While the injunction dealt with the felt threat of the CFTA, the ROM also defended itself by reiterating the pedagogical intent of *Into the Heart of Africa*. The news release announcing the injunction explained that the exhibit celebrates "the diverse cultures of many of Africa's peoples as well as provides thought-provoking insight into Canada's colonial past." But the ROM's discourse shifted in September 1990, after the Canadian Museum of Civilization in Quebec and the Vancouver Museum in British Columbia canceled their plans to host *Into the Heart of Africa*. Both of these museums cited "potential negative backlash" as their main reason for canceling the exhibit. A ROM news release issued in September 1990 stated:

> The ROM denies that the show is racist, and stands by the exhibition as a fair and careful investigation of that period of Canadian/African history. ... The exhibition neither endorses the attitudes of Canada's imperial past nor attempts to revise history by presenting something more palatable.

Here, the ROM defined *Into the Heart of Africa* in terms of its academic integrity, intellectual honesty, and neutrality. These themes were further developed in a news release issued November 28, 1990, when the Natural History Museum of Los Angeles County and the Albuquerque Museum in New Mexico canceled their plans to host *Into the Heart of Africa*:

> The controversy which surrounded this exhibition and led to the cancellation of the tour impinges on the freedom of all museums to maintain intellectual honesty, scientific and historical integrity, and academic freedom. Museums exist to determine objectively the record of nature and humanity.

This news release concluded with the statement that "the ROM will not be stampeded by controversy and will continue to present meaningful exhibitions which are challenging and truthful." John McNeill, the Acting Director of the ROM at the time, further pointed out that to succumb to fear of negative responses to any exhibit would result in "bland, or worse, misleading exhibitions and displays which express sanitized versions of history".[2] These statements focused attention on the tactics and rhetoric of the CFTA, but did not acknowledge any legitimacy in the CFTA's concerns about *Into the Heart of Africa* and the ROM.

It is interesting that in the above news releases, the ROM defined its work by using terms such as "objectivity" and "truth." This vocabulary reflects modernist claims that appeal to objectivity, neutrality, and scholarly disinterestedness (Giroux 1988: 14). In contrast, Cannizzo's background in cultural anthropology, and her specific interest in the ideological meanings of museum exhibits, are the product of a very different approach to knowledge. The theoretical perspective that informed *Into the Heart of Africa* challenges traditional ways of thinking about truth claims. Commenting on the implications of current theory, which Cannizzo is influenced by, Renato Rosaldo notes: "Terms such as objectivity, neutrality and impartiality refer to subject positions once endowed with great institutional authority, but now neither more nor less valid than those of more engaged yet equally perceptive social actors" (1989: 21). In contrast, the ROM news releases increasingly referred to notions of truth and objectivity in order to assert the museum's authority. Other perspectives, such as those of the CFTA, were subtly dismissed as partial, politicized, emotional, and nostalgic responses to "the truth," as represented by *Into the Heart of Africa*. The ROM's response to the CFTA was not unlike that of conservative critic Allan Bloom who, in his book *The Closing of the American Mind*, describes postmodernism as the "last predictable stage in the suppression of reason and the denial of the possibility of truth" (1987: 379). Once the four museums canceled their plans to receive *Into the Heart of Africa*, the ROM depicted the protestors as pursuing a "sanitized" version of history, and as suppressing academic freedom.

Curiously, despite her populist ideals, Cannizzo firmly planted herself on the side of institutional authority when, in an interview with curator Hazel Da Breo, she stated:

> The generation of scholarly aspects of the exhibition must be done by experts, however those experts are defined. For me, it's not a race issue, it's a question of expertise. Scholarly issues should be left in the hands of scholars, whoever those scholars are. (Cannizzo in Da Breo 1989/90: 37)

This type of defensive response toward the specter of sharing curatorial authority is not unusual among museum curators. As Stephen Weil points out, curators may "raise the claim of professional status as defense" against allowing community participation in exhibit design (1990: 2). Why this defensive posture? Following the pattern of Mary Douglas' analysis of pollution in *Purity and Danger* (1970), professionals fear that contributions by the public will dilute scholarly standards. Curators I interviewed also offered more specific reasons to explain why Cannizzo may have reacted the way she did. One anthropologist and curator noted that because Cannizzo was never granted tenure in a University, her sense of professional security was not solidified: "She's not really in the academic community. Perhaps this makes her need to claim academic privilege even stronger." The fact that Cannizzo was only a temporary curator at the ROM may have also intensified this reaction. As the above curator said, "Cannizzo is also an outsider at the ROM. All of this lack of security creates a certain amount of paranoia." Women academics appeared to be most sensitive to Cannizzo's "betwixt-and-between" position.

They tended to situate Cannizzo's fate in the context of the lack of security (financial and otherwise) that women in the academy experience (Aisenberg and Harrington 1988). On the other hand, both male and female professionals with whom I spoke repeatedly suggested that Cannizzo was not responsive enough to critiques and suggestions that a variety of people offered to her as the exhibit was being developed.

Classroom Confrontations

Shortly after *Into the Heart of Africa* closed at the ROM, Cannizzo was hired by the University of Toronto to teach an anthropology course called "Africa: Its Cultures and Peoples." In the classroom, Cannizzo faced many of the same students who had picketed *Into the Heart of Africa*, some of whom were not officially registered in the course. During the first two weeks of class, these students made announcements regarding the upcoming trial of the ROM protestors (the "ROM 11"), and the fact that *Into the Heart of Africa* was canceled by four major museums ("we should be grateful that this has happened," said one student (in O'Connell 1991: 13)). These aggressive remarks intensified in the third week of classes. This is how Julia Thompson, a student who was present and was not sympathetic to Cannizzo, described the atmosphere and events of this class:

> She was very, very nervous, extremely nervous. So her nervousness was a prod-
> uct of her own conscience and not a product of students' actions. My point is
> that with this charge of harassment by students, it was an internal harassment
> that was going on. It was not an external harassment. So in this class she was
> really nervous. There were a number of black students sitting in the back row,
> she wasn't looking up at the back row. She made a comment about black tribes
> and then she was very nervous with that word and she said, "well black groups,
> well it was black organizations." So she was really trying not to offend, trying to
> be politically correct. And a black student put up his hand and said, "I would
> really like to ask you a question. You're trying very hard to be politically correct
> now, you're being very careful not to offend. This summer when you put on the
> exhibit it didn't seem like you tried very hard at all and I'm wondering when this
> transformation took place." That was the question everybody wanted answered.
> (in O'Connell 1991: 13)

According to Paul Hamel, another student in the class, the situation quickly deteriorated into yelling when Cannizzo refused to answer the student's question. Hamel remembers Cannizzo being called a "fucking white supremist bitch" (in O'Connell 1991: 14). Cannizzo was followed out of the classroom and down the hall by the student who had questioned her (who may not have been enrolled in the class), and she eventually asked University Security to drive her home. She then faxed her resignation to the University of Toronto. This classroom confrontation is an apt example of what Cornel West (1992: 329) describes as an "escalation of the discourse of whiteness and blackness" and a "mentality of closing of ranks" that characterizes some versions of black nationalism. At this moment, it was difficult to imagine a space for dialogue.

Media Conclusions: Radicalizing the CFTA

Mainstream media reported these events in articles with sensationalist headlines such as "The pillorying of a curator" and "A surrender to vile harangues."[3] In the latter article, journalist Christie Blatchford in the Toronto Sun, commented on the cancellations of *Into the Heart of Africa*:

> What simply isn't bearable is that the cancellation of this tour is a victory for the yellers, the bully-boys who dogged the exhibition for at least half its run— staging their nasty shouting matches outside the museum every Saturday, throwing out the chilling "Racist" label at anyone who saw the show, or liked it, or even *didn't* like it—but believed in its right to exist. (1990)

In conclusion, Blatchford poses the question: "Why are we so bloody eager to be held hostage by the ravers from the political left? They won big on this one, you know." Despite its polemical tone, this article is representative of the way in which mainstream media increasingly characterized the CFTA as revisionists, bullies, blackmailers, "politically correct," "ravers from the political left," as "terrorists" and "intolerant".[4] Reiterating primitivist tropes, one article described the protestors as disrupting the "civilized" and "tolerant" atmosphere that classrooms deserve.[5] Cultural retrospectives published at the end of the year referred to the ROM controversy as an event indicative of the mood of our times. This mood was variously described as: "ill-tempered," "self-important, guilt-tripping, holier-than-thou and unforgiving," and as puritanical and zealous.[6]

Some journalists focused upon the protestors' apparent need to "sanitize the truth." This theme was considered, for example, by Peter Worthington in the *Ottawa Sun* in June 1990, during the early stages of the crisis. Worthington broaches the topic by way of analogy. He refers to the experiences of Amanda Lee Brooks, an historian who was discouraged by her doctoral advisor and by American black leaders because her research focused on the role of blacks in the slave trade. Brooks wrote a book on a woman slave trader named Madame Tinubu which, Worthington reports, was considered too controversial to publish.[7] In short, Brooks' experience serves as an example of Worthington's notion that "we avoid looking at history in the face these days. We are in an age of revisionist history—reshaping the past to make it more acceptable, fashionable, comfortable" (Worthington 1990). Dismissing the protestors' concerns about the exhibit, Worthington describes the show as "respectful, primitive, interesting, even artistic and memorable. I can't see real Africans being offended." He adds that "museums in Africa show a far more primitive past and don't duck historical truths." Finally, Worthington's piece is full of ironies, given Cannizzo's intentions. Perhaps this is the drama of the clash between universalizing, modernist conceptions of "the primitive" and "the civilized," and postmodernist pedagogic strategies of demystifying and opening up these traditions (see Foster 1983).

It was the depiction of the protestors as part of an emerging "politically correct" movement that eventually dominated journalistic commentaries about the ROM controversy.[8] In May 1991, *Maclean's* published a feature story called "The Silencers: 'Politically Correct' Crusaders are Stifling Expression and Behavior." The issue coincided with the 1991 Learned Societies Conference. The cover photograph shows two academics with gags over their mouths. The lead article by Tom Fennell was titled "The Silencers: A New Wave of Repression is Sweeping Through the Universities." Fennell claims that across North America, academics and others are being repressed by intellectuals and political activists who, in their battle against racism and sexism, stifle free speech. To support his argument, Fennell notes four incidents of supposed repression by politically correct forces. These include: black students' harassment of Jeanne Cannizzo at the University of Toronto, student protests against Phillipe Rushton at the University of Western Ontario, feminist students' protests against the reproduction of an Alex Colville painting at Acadia University, and protests against a Vancouver Shakespeare conference by a group of unidentified feminists.[9] In *Maclean's*, the issues surrounding Cannizzo's treatment are described in terms of a central tension between dominant white culture and minorities on campus. Paraphrasing Desmond Morton, President of the University of Toronto's Erindale campus, Fennel writes: "The University authorities did nothing to help Cannizzo because under a new, rapidly unfolding moral order, it is considered unacceptable for a white person to be critical of minority groups" (1991: 40). It is true that the Scarborough campus of the University of Toronto gave Cannizzo little support. Officials reportedly said that they were unaware of the fact that Cannizzo was the curator of *Into the Heart of Africa* when they hired her.[10] (This comment did not strike Professor Martin Klein, an Africanist and friend of Cannizzo who teaches at the downtown University of Toronto campus, as believable.) The Scarborough College Council did attempt to pass a motion to support Cannizzo and to welcome her back to the University if she chose to return. However, this motion was intensely debated during a packed council meeting, and finally a compromise motion was passed. The amended motion conveyed concern for Cannizzo and for the students in her anthropology course (concern for students' right to free expression influenced this amendment). Following the meeting, one academic apparently called the vote "the work of gutless liberal bastards" (O'Donnell 1991:18). And Ian Robertson, a Professor of Canadian History who was Chairperson of the College Council, submitted his resignation.

In contrast to the Scarborough Council, the University of Toronto's senior administration did support Cannizzo. In response to the classroom incident, University President Robert Pritchard announced: "As a university we are committed to freedom of speech and freedom of inquiry by both faculty and students. Abusive behavior in a classroom is a fundamental violation of both principles" (in Abbate 1990: 30). As well as defining the controversy as a freedom of speech issue, Robert Pritchard consulted with five senior social scientists and Africanists on faculty, gathering testimony that Cannizzo was qualified to teach a course on Africa, and that she was not racist.

Maclean's depiction of a politically correct movement sweeping across campuses (and museums, and the public school system) did not go uncontested. Michael Keefer (1992), for example, calls for a dose of skepticism vis-a-vis journalistic writing about the politically correct. Keefer argues that a small number of incidents have become icons of politically correct repression and are repeated ad nauseam in articles.[11] As well, the language used to describe the politically correct often verges on the hysterical. Historian Joan Wallach Scott notes that members of the National Association of Scholars (NAS) refer to the politically correct as the campus "thought police," and discuss the need to "fend off the "barbarians"" (an interesting primitivist trope) "who are storming the gates of academe and who would deprive us of our individual freedom" (1991: 34). Doug Smith, writing in *Canadian Dimension* (1991), points out the hypocrisy evident in some conservative critics who now pose as neutral defenders of free speech. For instance, while President George Bush spoke at the University of Michigan about the P.C. threat to free speech, Smith notes that the American Supreme Court under Bush restricted employees of federally funded clinics from mentioning abortion to clients and prohibited public sector unions from using union dues for political activities (1991: 10). After noting a variety of recent political events in the United States, Smith suggests that conservatives employ the term P.C. in order to dismiss complaints of minorities while appearing to favour free speech.

The Academy and Complex Subject-Positions

Many people who were critical of the way in which the CFTA were defined as "politically correct," were nevertheless genuinely disturbed by the harassment that Cannizzo experienced on campus. Thus, a number of journalists and academics carefully negotiated a position in which they expressed suspicion about the construction of the P.C. debates, while simultaneously criticizing the

CFTA. For instance, in his article entitled "The sinister crusade against 'politically correct'," Gerald Caplan positioned himself by noting:

> Certainly I agree absolutely that some PCers have gone unacceptably overboard in their quest for justice. Canada's most notorious example was the unfortunate attack on the Royal Ontario Museum for its exhibition called Into the Heart of Africa, and the subsequent witch hunt against its curator Jeanne Cannizzo. (1990: B3)

Michael Keefer, in his critique of the *Maclean's* coverage of the P.C. debates, adopts a similar posture. While he suggests that *Maclean's* exaggerates the threat of the "politically correct," Keefer is concerned by Cannizzo's harassment. He interprets this incident as an anomaly, rather than as representative of a trend sweeping across University campuses. He admits that the incident is a case where "over-zealous or injudicious opponents of racism, misogyny, and homophobia within the universities may have infringed upon the rights of other people" (Keefer 1992: 97). Such nuanced positions vis-a-vis the ROM controversy were rarely reported by the mainstream press. Clearly, the controversy gained a level of complexity when "victims" of racism became "aggressors" in the classroom. Once the CFTA harassed Cannizzo, their "moral power" (Dyck 1985: 190) was greatly diminished, particularly in the eyes of feminist scholars.

Women curators tended to identify strongly with the intimidation that Cannizzo experienced. Enid Schildkrout, for example, noted that in light of the ROM controversy, "many of us working in the field of ethnographic exhibitions, particularly African exhibitions, tremble with a sense of 'there but for the grace of God go I'" (1991: 16). Schildkrout curated a major exhibit entitled *African Reflections: Art from Northeastern Zaire* (1990), which showed at the Museum of Natural History in New York. A student of African art whom I interviewed told me that *African Reflections* was, in fact, picketed by black demonstrators. The demonstrations were, however, directed at raising awareness about current politics in Zaire. Marjorie Halpin, a curator with the Museum of Anthropology (MOA) in Vancouver and a cultural anthropologist, spoke of similar feelings of fear as she prepared an African exhibit called *Fragments: Reflections on Collecting* (1991). Constructed from an eclectic selection of passages from African novelists, poets and artists, as well as quotes from curators and historians, *Fragments* included a passage by Cannizzo on exhibiting culture. However, while Halpin may have been inspired by Cannizzo's writing, *Fragments* contrasted strongly with *Into the Heart of Africa* for the way in which it made strong connections with contemporary cultural productions and politics in Africa.

It was a serious challenge for academics who understand themselves (and their studies) as being anti-racist, to take a stand against the CFTA.

Michael Lambek expressed this challenge in the following way: "Our sympathy and solidarity with those who wish to eradicate racism should not allow us to disguise the fact that she [Cannizzo] has become the victim of persecution" (1990). A similar tension was expressed to me by Martin Klein, who publicly defended Cannizzo's academic reputation: "Some of my students were on the opposite side. I ordinarily might have had misgivings about my black constituency but I felt that the morality of what was happening was so important that I had to [support Cannizzo]." Clearly, the ROM controversy pushed both Lambek and Klein into the uncomfortable position of recognizing that victims of racism can also be guilty of racism. Both Lambek and Klein decided against supporting weak arguments, even if they were directed toward good causes. Gates (1992a: 35) also argues for this kind of vigilance toward the way in which debates are constructed.

Curator Hazel Da Breo also experienced the controversy surrounding *Into the Heart of Africa* as personally challenging. When the protests of *Into the Heart of Africa* began, Global TV arranged to interview her, along with Cannizzo and the CFTA. Da Breo felt confident that in this context she would be able to clearly articulate her ambivalent feelings about *Into the Heart of Africa*. However, this did not occur. The CFTA did not participate in the interview, and Da Breo found that clips of her interview were strategically juxtaposed with the interview with Cannizzo. She remembers watching Global TV after the interview and experiencing a sense of not recognizing herself. Portrayed as radically opposed to *Into the Heart of Africa*, Da Breo received congratulatory phone calls the next day from members of the CFTA. This experience was very painful for Da Breo, as she felt as though the complexity and texture of her thoughts, and her professional respect for Cannizzo, were misrepresented.

Each of these examples illustrate the extent to which the ROM controversy was not a static debate between blacks and whites or between the left and right. Rather, the ROM controversy challenged people to construct their identities, while at the same time they were being constructed by others.

The Black Community: "Protest and Process"

Members of the black community in Toronto also defined themselves in relation, and sometimes in opposition to the CFTA. Responses of the Black Business and Professional Association (BBPA) to the CFTA were particularly interesting from the point of view of considering how class issues intersected with discourses of race. The BBPA has a membership that includes many successful and prominent professionals, and is therefore oriented towards the establishment, as well as the larger black community. An article entitled "Protest and Process," published in a June 1990 BBPA newsletter, offers a sense of the BBPA's values and goals. Without naming the CFTA, this article discusses how the BBPA can work productively and co-operatively with groups more radical than itself:

> For a long time in the Black Community we have had two solitudes. There are those who protest publicly and vocally against the prejudices, injustices and discriminations of the society. They march and demonstrate when a Black person is shot by police, or an institution, such as the Royal Ontario Museum, mounts an exhibition that they consider to be racist. Then there are those, who in response to the same incidents and situation, engage in a process of quiet dialogue and debate, seeking common interest, and persuading change.
>
> Traditionally those who protest have dismissed those involved in the process as ineffectual compromisers without commitment who don't understand the reality of the struggle. And, those who work the process traditionally dismiss the protestors as irresponsible loudmouths who simply aggravate the situation. The powers who discriminate and perpetuate the prejudices and injustices, look at this division and exploit it. They woo those committed to quiet dialogue, and deplore the excesses of protest. Then they engage in endless talks with little outcome. They sometimes react to the protestors with mock concern and vague promises, but ride out the crisis expecting little follow up until the next crisis.
>
> The answer is simple. Both groups are concerned about the same things; EQUITY and JUSTICE, and upset and outraged by the same things; INEQUITY AND INJUSTICE. Their methodologies differ. But if they get together and coordinate, those methodologies become complementary to serve the same goals. When the powers want to talk to "responsible leaders" we go jointly with common concerns and common commitments. If we are not divided, then we are that much harder to rule and manipulate.

This excerpt provides a useful backdrop for considering relations between the CFTA and the BBPA during the ROM controversy. The BBPA attempted to act as a mediator between the CFTA and the ROM, with largely unsuccessful results. While the BBPA attempted to create opportunities for dialogue between the ROM and the CFTA (and their respective lawyers), the CFTA refused any form of negotiation or compromise.[12] The CFTA asserted that "a pre-condition for any talks was the dismantling of the exhibition."

On June 1, 1990, a Town Meeting for the black community was held. This was organized by the BBPA, who had approached the Black Action Defense Committee (BADC) to help bring together a broad spectrum of people to identify common concerns. While Rico raised the ROM issue at the meeting, it was largely overshadowed by other issues such as "many aspects of police/community relations; ideas for using Caribbana to make a stronger political and cultural statement; and the need for support programs for the vulnerable in the Black community." The next day, June 2, 1990, the CFTA clashed with police. Following this incident, Carl Masters of the BBPA arranged a meeting with the

ROM, however the CFTA did not attend. This was the first of a number of unsuccessful attempts to create space for a dialogue between the CFTA, the BBPA, and the ROM. The CFTA worked with the following demands:

1. Dismantle the exhibition,
2. Admit it was racist and apologize for this,
3. Undertake to get prior approval from the Black community on the form and content of future exhibitions about Africa or Black people,
4. Hire more Black consultants and staff,
5. Include Black people on the Board of Directors.

While the ROM would not agree to these first three demands, it accepted the principle of consultation, and stated that the other issues concerning representation were negotiable. It is important to note that CFTA concerns about representation within the ROM were rarely reported in the media. This is a critical point, and one which enters most discussions about the relationship of museums to knowledge and power. As Donald Garfield summarizes:

> A substantial amount of scholarship—and a proliferation of high-profile professional conferences—reflects the museum community's awareness that everything from exhibitions to staffing and board composition needs to be scrutinized if museums as social and cultural institutions are to adapt to the radical changes occurring in U.S. society. (1989: 43)

Although Garfield refers to the American context, his comment seems highly relevant to the Canadian one, which, like its American counterpart, is becoming increasingly multicultural.[13]

At a second Town Meeting on July 6, 1990, CFTA member Gerald Phokohye made the following motion:

> Whereas the ROM situation is of serious concern; the exhibition is a racist insult; and the CFTA struggle is anti-racist, be it resolved:
>
> 1. To congratulate the CFTA,
> 2. To condemn the ROM for a racist exhibition,
> 3. To express solidarity with the 11 demonstrators arrested and charged,
> 4. To call on the ROM to have charges dropped,
> 5. To pledge financial support for the CFTA, and
> 6. To ask Black media to give positive coverage of the situation.

Approximately one third of those present voted in favour while the remainder abstained (there were approximately 160 people present). This vote is an indicator of the ambivalence (or perhaps indifference) that people felt towards the CFTA and the ROM controversy despite CFTA claims otherwise.

This issue of difference within the black community was further addressed by the BBPA in a press release dated August 6, 1990. The statement addressed the CFTA's claims to represent the entire black community. It noted that there was in fact a wide range of opinions about *Into the Heart of Africa* within the black community. It further suggested that the CFTA's claim to be a broad based coalition was inaccurate. Out of a list of twenty groups claiming to support the CFTA, only five were listed in the Black Secretariat directory. The remaining fifteen groups, including the African and Caribbean Student Association (ACSA) gave their addresses as c/o ACSA. This information suggests that the CFTA was broadly student and youth-based.

The BBPA did not criticize the actions of the CFTA, but rather its claims to represent the entire community. In fact, relations between the BBPA and the CFTA deteriorated further when members of the ACSA (claiming to act on behalf of the CFTA) broke up the third Town Meeting on August 10, 1990.

These incidents reflect the extent to which the politics of the CFTA were essentially separatist (some people I interviewed thought that some members of the CFTA were affiliated with Louis Farrakan, an association that would seem to fit the more militant expressions within the CFTA). Dwight Whylie, who was Vice-President of the BBPA at the time, described to me how the CFTA called the BBPA "lackies of the establishment and lickers of white boots." Despite the BBPA's interest in community issues and black empowerment, they were constructed by the CFTA as too integrated and connected to the dominant establishment. Certainly, this can be a painful position in which to find oneself (see Early 1992). Finally, like many academics, members of the BBPA constructed contingent and complex relations with the CFTA.

Victims and Victimization

When Trilby Bittle, the Head of Marketing and Public Information at the ROM, provided me with roughly 150 newspaper articles documenting the ROM controversy, it was interesting to note that all of the articles but one referred directly to *Into the Heart of Africa*. The single unrelated piece was "Don't Blame Me!: The New Culture of Victimization," written by John Taylor and published in *New York* (1991). Bittle explained to me that the article would provide a useful context for thinking about what happened at the ROM. Let us briefly read the ROM crisis in light of the "culture of victimization."

Taylor describes the culture of victimization as the growing compulsion among Americans of all "creeds, colors, and incomes, of the young and the old, the infirm and the robust, the guilty as well as the innocent, to ascribe to themselves the status of victims to try to find someone or something else to blame for whatever is wrong or incomplete or just plain unpleasant about their lives" (1991: 28). To develop this idea, Taylor refers to a potpourri of examples ranging from the case of Rose Cipollone, who contracted lung cancer after 40 years of heavy smoking and proceeded to sue three tobacco companies, to the case of Dan White, who murdered San Francisco mayor George Moscone and claimed that eating junk food had caused him to go temporarily insane. Lumped together with these stories of individual complaints is a brief reference to ACT UP's declaration that AIDS victims are dying not only from AIDS, but also from the lack of government commitment to finding a cure for AIDS. Finally, Taylor (1991: 33) discusses "racial victimization," suggesting that American blacks are "perennial victims"—people who are both victimized by racism, and who simultaneously use their status as victims as a source of power. Taylor refers to conservative critic Shelby Steele, particularly Steele's view of affirmative action as a failed program that serves only to reward and reinforce victimization. The subtext to Steele's argument is that blacks exploit white guilt and manipulate their status as victims.

It is not difficult to read the ROM controversy in light of Taylor's analysis. Taylor would say that the CFTA acted out and exploited their victimization. The problem with this perspective is that it does not recognize the legitimacy of the grievances or demands expressed by the CFTA. If Bittle or any other ROM employees identified with this argument, then they likely felt that the ROM was a victim of the controversy.

Other Voices at the ROM

Significantly, some employees of the ROM questioned mainstream media interpretations of the controversy and the ROM's manner of responding to the protestors. Rather than reduce Cannizzo and the ROM to victims of politically correct forces, these museum professionals developed more textured and self-critical accounts of the controversy. These employees were not, however, apologists for the CFTA. Like many academics, their relationship with the ROM, Cannizzo, and the CFTA was multi-layered and contingent. By considering these employees' perspectives on the controversy we can appreciate that the ROM is no monolithic power, even if it appeared that way in the media. We can also gain new perspectives on the controversy and the museological issues at stake in it.

Museum professionals' critiques of the ROM focused on two themes. First, concern was expressed over the fact that for many members of the black community, *Into the Heart of Africa* was neither effective nor enjoyable. Second, some employees felt that the ROM responded to the protests too defensively. The ROM's lack of success in dealing with members of the black community was often linked to its internal structure and ethos. Like many critics from without, these ROM employees perceived the ROM to be bureaucratic, hierarchical, and representative of the interests of the status quo.

Within the ROM, one site of internal resistance is represented by a report by the Exhibits Design Division entitled "*Into the Heart of Africa*: An Evaluation" (Crawford, Hankel and Rowse 1990).[14] This evaluation of *Into the Heart of Africa* is based on audience research that was conducted during, and in response to, the controversy. The research team carried out this research by interviewing individual visitors and tour groups, as well as by observing (or "tracking") visitors as they viewed *Into the Heart of Africa*. Data collected covered a variety of subjects: socio-economic and ethnic profiles of the visitors; expectations about the subject of the exhibit; reactions to the exhibit title; perceptions of the central message of the exhibit; and general impressions (likes and dislikes) related to the exhibit. This evaluation reveals the wide variety of interpretations that visitors made of *Into the Heart of Africa*. In particular, the researchers expressed concerns that Cannizzo's anti-racist intentions were misread. Posing the question of how the *Into the Heart of Africa* controversy might have been avoided, the study concludes that the ROM did not have enough knowledge about the interests and concerns of members of the black community. To counter this knowledge gap, the study recommends that the ROM develop practices of community consultation. In particular, the authors state that had audience research been conducted by the ROM before developing *Into the Heart of Africa*, a more effective and sensitive exhibit could have been developed.

Unfortunately, staff members I spoke with generally felt that the ROM was unsupportive of audience research and community consultation. Apparently, the evaluation of *Into the Heart of Africa* was not well received by senior administration within the ROM. Moreover, although the evaluation was originally intended to be a public document, ROM Director John McNeill decided that it should only be internally circulated.

For Leslie Patten, the past Assistant Head in Exhibit Design Services, the ROM's lack of support for audience research was part of a larger ideological struggle within the ROM between the "hard" sciences (represented by Director John McNeill) and the social sciences. According to Patten, staff who were committed to qualitative audience research and community consultation felt undervalued by the ROM, resulting in an exodus of senior staff that began in the Summer of 1990 and continued for approximately 18 to 24 months. For these staff members, contestation over *Into the Heart of Africa* was part of a larger institutional struggle.

Many staff members were also critical of the way in which the ROM responded to the demonstrators. They were concerned by the fact that the ROM focused on managing and containing the protestors of *Into the Heart of Africa*, rather than adopting a more self-reflexive perspective. According to one senior staff member, most ROM board members reacted to the CFTA with fear, "as if the ROM were under a state of siege." However, the board did not critically examine its own role in allowing the controversy around

Into the Heart of Africa to develop. Questions such as why early warnings about the exhibit were ignored were not addressed.

This lack of self-criticism occurred partly as a result of the structure and practices of the ROM board. Decision-making rarely takes place at the board level; rather, the executive committee and other working committees tend to make decisions. Consequently, votes taken at board meetings usually have an air of fait accompli. One consequence of this practice is that issues are rarely debated in an in-depth manner. Thus, in the case of *Into the Heart of Africa*, board members did not critically review their role and accountability in the controversy. As curator David Pendergast explained: "The one thing that wasn't ever addressed in my hearing at least, in a board meeting or anywhere else in the museum as far as I'm aware, was the obvious failure of the system, the structure within which decisions were made about the show." Consequently, some staff members felt that the board distanced itself from the controversy, subtly directing the controversy toward Cannizzo. A comment by a member of the CFTA supports this interpretation of the ROM's political strategy:

> The museum is the museum, right. It's a faceless thing. And she was a concrete person. So if you're lashing out against something, an institution, it's faceless. But she is there. She's the one whose name is on the brochure. She's the one whose name is on the thing, curated by such and such. She's a live, a visible person. So of course she would be the natural target if you will.

In contrast with this scenario, Pendergast suggested that the ROM should have adopted a more self-critical stance vis-a-vis *Into the Heart of Africa*:

> I think the museum showed a considerable lack of courage to come out and say, in light of all this, we have reviewed the show and we agree that there are areas there that probably should not have been put together the way they were, and one could come away with a confused message or an incomplete message, and that was an error in design. And that error was partly the work of the curator responsible for the exhibition, but it was also our responsibility.

This imagined and constructive response to the controversy contrasts sharply with the ROM's authoritative posture discussed earlier.

Outcomes

It is important to consider the impact of the CFTA on the ROM. In theoretical terms, this means considering the relationship of the event (the controversy) to the enduring social structure (the ROM). Have changes in practice occurred? What wisdom has been culled from the controversy?

Following *Into the Heart of Africa* the ROM did attempt to establish a consultation process with members of the black community. An Advisory

Committee, which included a number of members of the BBPA, was established to help with the design and presentation of *Caribbean Celebrations*, which showed at the ROM from June 6 till September 3, 1991. The Advisory Committee urged the ROM to make a public, conciliatory statement about *Into the Heart of Africa*, and this statement became a major source of contestation. On March 1, 1991, John McNeill issued a conciliatory letter, in which he stated: "Racism has no place in any of our society's institutions, public or private, and the ROM emphasizes that the show was developed with academic integrity and was not intended to offend or hurt any race or group. In this context, the ROM expressed its regret for any offence that was felt over the exhibition." In this letter, McNeill also quoted Thomas Kierans, Chair of the ROM's Board of Trustees as saying, "I don't think the ROM did anything wrong, but it missed an opportunity to bond with an important part of the community. It is still very painful because we are not above the community, we are part of the community." As well, the letter announced that a joint Staff-Trustee Committee on Community Relationships had been established, and that part of its mandate would be to examine the ROM's hiring practices.

This letter was not well received by the Advisory Committee, since it did not acknowledge the legitimacy of concerns of protestors of *Into the Heart of Africa*. On March 8, 1991, the Advisory Committee issued a statement in response to the ROM: "We regret that Dr. McNeill continues to state the erroneous view that the objection of members of the Black community and many others of conscience to last summer's exhibition was unwarranted and that the ROM was blameless." In particular, McNeill's statement was a source of concern since its wording was different than committee members had expected. As Keith Ellis, a member of the Advisory Committee stated: "We spoke of the harm that was caused in our community, the museum spoke of harm that was felt."[15] Finally, in June 1991, the apology issue was resolved. In a news release, the ROM stated its regret "for any offence unintentionally caused to members of the African Canadian community and to other groups and individuals." Following this strained community consultation process, *Caribbean Celebrations* turned out to be a successful (and uncontroversial) exhibit.

Other significant developments at the ROM include the appointment of Keith Ellis to the Board of Directors and the opening of the Egypt/Nubia gallery in January 1992. The gallery's recognition of Nubia, and its examination of the relationship of Nubia to Egypt, is a bold initiative within the field of museology. The gallery is relevant to current debates about the politics of knowledge, particularly the way in which the history of Western Civilization is represented (see Wilford 1992).

Finally, while more members of the black community are now involved with the ROM than before *Into the Heart of Africa*, it would be naive to assume that issues concerning knowledge and power are now easily resolved.

There are members of the black community who have no interest in working with the ROM, and there are board members at the ROM who want to avoid contact with "vocal" minorities. But, I think it is fair to say that the ROM is no longer a revered "temple." There seems to be an increased awareness that representations of history are contingent and therefore open to debate. This became vivid to me when I visited the Egypt/Nubia gallery. A display on adornment featured a mannequin of an Egyptian woman applying cosmetics. An interpreter stationed next to this display held a sample of the type of rock from which these cosmetics would have been fashioned.[16] Visitors held the rock and asked her questions. Did all Egyptian women wear cosmetics? What was the life span of an Egyptian woman? Is this how an Egyptian woman really looked? In response to this last question, the interpreter discreetly replied: "Well, this is how *they* say she looked." She further explained to me that this display was strictly the ROM's interpretation, and that personally, she felt that the woman looked too white. Indeed, the color of the mannequin's skin was white and her features were noticeably Caucasian. With a certain complicity and a sense of humour, we agreed that the mannequin looked like I do, and not, it went without saying, like the interpreter who was black.

Welsh poet Dylan Thomas is famous for walking into a dusty museum in his home town and pronouncing, "This museum ought to be in a museum" (Morris in Ames 1992: 15). Fortunately, my excursion into the ROM's Egypt/Nubia galley did not produce this familiar somnolent effect that can occur in museums that insist upon formality and univocal narratives. The subtle contestations over representation that I encountered proved to be provocative and memorable.

Afterword

The controversy surrounding *Into the Heart of Africa* has become, during the past few years, a touchstone for discussions about the possibilities and limitations of reflexive museology, and about post-colonial and multicultural identity politics. Is it possible, for example, to mount a critical and reflexive exhibit from within an establishment museum such as the ROM? Further, can such an exhibit be accessible to a wide audience? For many critics of *Into the Heart of Africa* the answer to these questions is a resounding no. In fact, *Into the Heart of Africa* has been canonized as a quintessential example of postmodernism's conservatism and elitism. For instance, in her analysis of the controversy connected with the show, Eva Mackey (1995) suggests that postmodernism provides elite cultural producers with tools for protecting their own power. Mackey's argument is compelling, but it does not leave room to consider how Cannizzo was made vulnerable by the controversy, or for examining ways in which irony and reflexivity can be empowering for minorities.

Irony has the potential to be an important tool for exposing contradictions between society's ideals and practices, and for subverting dominant conventions. A particularly relevant example is *Fluffs and Feathers: An Exhibition on the Symbols of Indianness*, which showed at the ROM from November 1992 until February 1993. *Fluffs and Feathers* examined stereotypes of Natives in popular culture, presenting artifacts such as book illustrations, advertisements, souvenirs, and Hollywood movie posters. The exhibit was very successful, but it is important to note that its conditions of production were very different than those of *Into the Heart of Africa*. While *Into the Heart of Africa* was produced by the ROM (and with no real community consultation),

97

Fluffs and Feathers was produced by the Woodland Cultural Centre in Brantford, Ontario, where it was guest curated by Deborah Doxtator. Thus, while *Into the Heart of Africa* was associated with the ROM (read, the status quo), *Fluffs and Feathers* was associated with a local First Nations setting (Doxtator 1993). This made its politics clear—there was no danger of its reflexivity being read as nostalgic, as opposed to oppositional.

Marlene Nourbese Philip's narrative *Looking for Livingstone: An Odyssey of Silence* (1990) is another strong example of how irony can succeed as a form of resistance. I want to briefly discuss *Looking for Livingstone* since it appears to be a response to *Into the Heart of Africa*. Philip was an active and influential critic of the exhibit.) In *Looking for Livingstone*, a narrator travels alone through Africa, following, as she says, in Livingstone's footsteps. Along the way, she encounters tribal peoples and learns about their silences. Of her own silence, she explains that Livingstone "discovered silence—my silence—discovered it, owned it, possessed it like it was never possessed before" (Philip 1990: 20). But the narrator is determined to cure herself of Dr. Livingstone, this man who supposedly made history. Deconstructing the very idea of "discovery," she writes:

> David Livingstone, Dr. David Livingstone, 1813–73—Scottish, not English, and one of the first Europeans to cross the Kalahari—with the help of the Bushmen; was shown the Zambezi by the indigenous African and "discovered" it and renamed it. Victoria Falls. Then he set out to "discover" the source of the Nile and was himself "discovered" by Stanley—"Dr. Livingstone, I presume?" And History. Stanley and Livingstone—white fathers of the continent. Of silence. (1991: 7)

This piece offers a sense of the opportunities that Cannizzo seems to have missed in terms of explicitly deconstructing the photographs re-presented in *Into the Heart of Africa*. For instance, Cannizzo presented, but did not comment upon, an engraving of "Livingstone's discovery of Lake Nyasa," reproduced from *Heroes of the Dark Continent* by J. W. Buel.[1]

After a long journey, the traveler in *Looking for Livingstone* encounters what she calls the "Museum of Silence." We learn that this museum has been "erected to house the many and varied silences of different peoples" (1990: 57). In this museum, the traveler finds her silence, carefully guarded in an exhibit case. She reflects: "My silence was now a structure, an edifice I could walk around, touch, feel, lick even—and I did—it was cold, cold to the tongue. I could if I wanted, even pee on it, though that would be difficult, contained as it was behind plexiglass" (1990: 57–8). Here, Philip parodies and subverts the image of the museum as temple, a site of authority, reverence, and orderly conduct. Her play on the idea of the Museum of Silence, and on being silenced evokes a strong sense of the politics of exhibiting culture. She confronts the curator of this museum: "It was mine—ours—I challenged, to do with as we please—to destroy if we so wanted. They told me the silences were best kept where they could be labelled, annotated, dated and catalogued—"in such and such a year, this piece of silence was taken from the ____" (1990: 57). This passage is evocative of the ROM controversy, where protestors claimed the right to control representations of African culture.

Both *Fluffs and Feathers* and *Looking for Livingstone* suggest that irony can be not only oppositional, but also accessible. This was also illustrated by my discussion of Wilson's *The Other Museum* in Chapter Two. As well, these examples suggest that reflexive museology can raise questions of appropriation and exploitation in a direct way. It is surely a loss that *Into the Heart of Africa* did not succeed in this regard.

It is not difficult to imagine curatorial strategies that Cannizzo could have employed in order to meet her goals of creating a critical exhibit about colonialism and collecting: the inclusion of African voices and post-colonial cultural productions; an exploration of how African Canadians relate to the ROM's African collection; the use of images of resistance to colonialism's logic and gaze; the creation of linkages with local black museums; a broadening of the authoring base of the exhibit.[2]

Museum professionals, including Cannizzo, have issued foreboding warnings about the *Into the Heart of Africa* controversy, suggesting it represents a case of the suppression of academic freedom. As discussed in the previous chapter, this analysis fails to recognize the legitimacy of protestors' concerns, or their right to participate in public culture. The focus on the specter of the loss of academic freedom also fails to adequately appreciate the extent to which museums have a tendency to contain and domesticate radical interventions.[3] It is, however, possible that the *Into the Heart of Africa* controversy will lead to self-censorship and the production of less experimental, more controlled exhibits. Certainly, this appears to be the case with the London Portrait Gallery's recent exhibit, to which Cannizzo contributed, entitled *David Livingstone and the Victorian Encounter with Africa* (1996). While the exhibit had many elements that were similar to *Into the Heart of Africa*— including the lantern slide show and a chance to win a safari—it had a quality of restraint and control that the former did not have. It was inoffensive and veered away from provocation. It was a quiet exhibit; symbolic of this is the fact that the lantern show no longer included a recording of Cannizzo's voice. But despite predictions about the rise in self-censorship amongst curators in an age of political correctness and conservative government interventions (witness the dilution of the Enola Gay exhibit at the Smithsonian), I am confident that there is plenty of space for provocative and brilliant exhibits.

This leaves me with one final concern about *Into the Heart of Africa*, which is the extent to which questions concerning racism and "institution-building around specific ethnic identities and histories" (Ruffins 1997: 80) have tended to be ignored in debates about the controversy.[4] Although little work has been done in this area, there is a general sense that processes leading to the decolonization of museums are accelerating in relation to indigenous minorities in countries such as Australia, New Zealand, Canada, and the United States (Harrison 1993; Simpson 1996). Africans in the diaspora do not have comparable partnerships with mainstream museums.[5] The different impacts of the controversies surrounding *The Spirit Sings* and *Into the Heart of Africa* in Canada illustrate this point. *The Spirit Sings* boycott generated a national conference called "Preserving our Heritage" (1988), which was organized jointly by the Assembly of First Nations and the Canadian Museums Association. This in turn led to the formation of a national task force organized by the same two groups, which produced a report entitled "Turning the Page: Forging New Partnerships Between Museums and First Peoples" (1992). In contrast, there was no comparable follow-up to the controversy surrounding *Into the Heart of Africa*. This means that public debates about issues related to historical and contemporary racism and the meaning of blackness in multicultural societies were not sustained by protestors, critics, or museum professionals. This is unfortunate given that debates about the shape and texture of post-colonial societies need to occur. Finally, the fact that *Into the Heart of Africa* did not travel, represents a lost opportunity in terms of creating sites that generate debate about the legacies of colonialism and contemporary identity politics. Such practices encourage museum visitors to see beyond themselves, and to understand their own history and identity in relation to others. In this way, the museum is not only a site of affirmation, but also a place where complex histories can be continually produced, contested, and negotiated. Ethnographies of museums can enable us to appreciate the charged politics and rich poetics that characterize these negotiations. Following this, it becomes possible to appreciate both legacies and possibilities of exhibiting and performing culture.

Appendix: Coalition for the Truth about Africa Pamphlet

The Truth About Africa

This pamphlet is not designed to sell you on any new product or idea, neither is it to turn you against the Royal Ontario Museum. This pamphlet is to inform you of a great injustice being brought against humanity.

The ROM is currently presenting an exhibit entitled "Into the Heart of Africa." An exhibit, which according to the ROM, is a portrayal of African history. Yet the exhibit represents a clear and concise attempt to mislead the public and to further tarnish the image of Africa and African people.

The entire world, museums, curators, et al. have become aware of the immense contributions made by Africa, and by people of African heritage to humanity. These gifts have been made from the dawn of time in every area of creativity—in the mart of action and in the sphere of thought. These contributions have continued even under situations of the gravest duress which Africa, and people of African descent have experienced in the last five hundred years.

Without any doubt, the ROM must be aware of these experiences and contributions of Africa, and Africans. How then, can the ROM carry such trite and condescending texts as found within this exhibit?

For example, there is a scene with four African women and one European woman. The depiction states that this is a scene of a white woman supervising the washing of four black women. Did Africans not know how to wash before the arrival of Europeans? There are also implicit and explicit, subliminal and obvious statements and suggestions of Europeans civilizing and developing Africa.

Terms like "Savage" and "Dark Continent" are buzz words of this sad and disgraceful presentation. What should have been made clear was that the role of the missionaries, like that of the soldiers, was to be agents of the Crown. The Crown was acting on the behalf of the colonial industry. In short, the Holy Trinity in Africa, no disrespect intended, was made up, not of the "Father, Son, and Holy Ghost," but instead, "The Missionary, Mercenary, and Merchant." It is folly to state or suggest that invaders such as Dr. Livingstone were heros of the African people.

To further illustrate to you the unfortunate miseducation which institutions such as the ROM have induced on ourselves and our children we would like to present a short listing of some of the gifts that the African civilization has endowed upon humanity. It is our hope that you may be enlightened by this information and help us in urging the ROM and such institutions in discontinuing to exhibit African history in such a deceitful manner.

Creators of Medicine

"During the millennia, Blacks in ancient Egypt made numerous contributions to medicine and were acknowledged as the inventors of the art of medicine. They produced the earliest physicians, medical knowledge, and medical literature. They contributed to the development of medicine in ancient Greece. Ancient writers affirm this."

Fredrick Newsome M.D., Journal of African Contributions

Creators of Art

"The first artist was Black. The oldest sculpture in the world, the 'Bas-Relief of White Rhinoceros with Ticks' was found in South Africa."

J. A. Rogers, Sex and Race Vol.1

Creators of Science

"Socrates (a black African), in the Phaidros, called the Egyptian god Thoth, the inventor of writing, astronomy, and geometry. Herodotus had a similarly high opinion of Egyptian science, stating that Greeks learned geometry from the Egyptians."

Dr. John Papperdemos, Professor of Physics,
University of Illinois

Creators of Astronomy

"The complex knowledge of the Dogon of Mali about the Sinus star system is sending shock waves around the scientific world. The West African people have not only plotted the orbits of the stars circling Sinus, but have revealed the extraordinary nature of one of the densest and tiniest stars in our galaxy. What is most astonishing about their revelations is that Sinus B is invisible to the unaided eye."

Hunter Adams III, African Observers of the Universe

"As early as 300 B.C., Africans built an astronomical site at Namoratunga in Northwestern Kenya and an accurate and complex pre-historic calendar, based on its astronomical alignments was developed in East Africa."

Godlrey C. Burns M.D., Journal of African Civilizations

Architecture

"It seems that the knowledge of mathematics and astronomy among the ancient Egyptians was considerably more extensive and exact than we had been led to suspect. The height of the Great Pyramid is one-billionth of the distance from Earth to the Sun, a unit of measurement not accurately established until 1974."

John Jackson, Introduction to African Civilization

- The pyramid is truly square, the sides being equal and angles being right angles.
- The four sockets on which the first four stones of the corners rested are on the same level.
- The directions of the sides are accurately to the four cardinal points.
- The vertical height of the pyramid bears the same proportion to its circumference at the base as the radius of a circle does to its circumference.

"The helical rising of Sinus was so important to the ancient Egyptians that gigantic temples were constructed with their main aisles oriented precisely towards the spot on the horizon where Sinus would appear on the expecteó morning. The light from Sirius would be channelled along the corridor (due to precise orientation) to flood the altar in the inner sanctums as it a pin-pointed spotlight had been switched on."

Mathematics

"The Rhind Papyrus shows that the Egyptians did invent arithmetic and geometric progressions."
"The Egyptians invented algebra."

Dr. Diop. The Nile Valley Civilization

Papyrus means paper, another African invention.

"Euclid of Alexandria, one of the greatest mathematicians of his era, lived (was born) and died in Africa. There is nothing to suggest that he ever left Africa."

Professor Lumpkin, The Nile Valley Civilizations

Alexandria was an Egyptian city, founded in 332 B.C.

Religion

"The earliest deities were woolly haired negroes. The pepper corn hair was a sign of divinity."

J. A. Rogers, 100 Amazing Facts about the Negro

"All religions originated in Africa."

Count C. F. Volney, Ruins of Empire

"The Greeks and Romans believed that their religion came from Egyptian religion up until about 100 A.D. Furthermore, Egyptian religion survives in Christianity itself. It is more accurate to view Christianity as a Judæo-Greek religion, though the New Testament was written in Greek and was influenced by Greek culture."

Lawrence E. Carter, The Nile Valley Civilizations

"The first gods (deities) of antiquity, from Greece to Mexico, were black Africans. The Ancients viewed the sacred image of divine as Black and the holy race of gods as Africans."

Black (African) gods

- Zeus of Greece
- Appollo of Greece
- Ostris of Egypt
- Isls of Rome
- Fuhl of China

- Buddha of India
- Horus of Rome
- Zaha of Japan
- Queztalcoatl of Mexico
- Krishna of India

Historically, religious figures such as Jesus Christ and the Prophet Mohammad are also commonly depicted as a Black Africans.

African Steel Making

"Researchers demonstrate evidence of a pre-historic, iron smelting technology that produced steel 1500 to 2000 years before Europe."

Godfrey C. Burns, Early African Sciences

"The temperature achieved in the blast furnace of the African steel making machine was higher than any achieved in a European machine until modern times. It was roughly 1,800°C, some 200 to 400°C higher than the highest reached in European cold blast bloomeries."

Edited by Ivan Van Sertima, Blacks in Science

And The List Goes On …

There are hundreds of documents and articles to draw from which prove that the African gift to humanity has been one of intellect, compassion and enlightenment and not of ignorance.

It is plain to see that the ROM has somehow *neglected* Africa's contribution to humanity within this exhibit and has instead opted to emphasize the demise of Africa and African people. They also have purposefully left out African's mouth piece, Egypt. We cannot blame the ROM alone though, such lies and misrepresentations have been told for hundreds of years. Do you remember Tarzan?

Our difficulty with the ROM is not with their carrying an African exhibit, but with the remarks accompanying these paintings, carvings, photos, etc. This exhibit thus reminds us too vividly of a past that is still not past.

Members of the African community contacted the curator, and director of the ROM indicating our willingness to assist with the exhibit. We have artists, art historians, anthropologists, and people with a variety of skills who could assist if the ROM wanted to be more sensitive and objective in its presentations and representations. We requested that:

(a) They exhibit the objects, but change the theme, or
(b) They close the show.

So far, their response, in writing has been insulting, and ineffectual. We therefore, request of the public, the following:

(a) That you avoid the exhibit, or if you go, visit on thursdays and note discrepancies, and draw them to the attention of the ROM.
(b) You contact a library or bookstore and get material that could enhance your knowledge of Africa.

Among some of the publications we recommend are:

Walter Rodney, How Europe Underdeveloped Africa,
George G. M. James, Stolen Legacy
Chelkh Anta Dlop, African origins of Civilization.

There are several other books for all ages, as well as libraries and bookstores where these are available, like the Third World Bookstore. The ROM receives the support of our people. We respect institutions that attempt to humanize and to educate the public, especially the children. It is our responsibility to ensure that our past is well represented for the sake of generations to come. All children, of every race, may only benefit from the truth being told. But no child can truly benefit from lies or deceit.

This pamphlet is brought to you by The Coalition for the Truth About Africa which consists of the following supporting and endorsing organizations: African & Caribbean Student Association (ACSA), African & Caribbean Student Collective (of Toronto), Black Heritage Association, Black Meres, Caribbean Student Association (York University), Daughters in Africa, Kenya Human Rights Organization (Canada), Negus Educational Foundation, Rally Against Apartheld, Riddim (Radio CIUT), Sister Vision Press. The African Caribbean Club (Humber College), The African Resource Centre, The Black Woman's Collective of U of T, O.S.I.E., UJAMAA, United Coalition Against Racism, Unity Force, Woman's Coalition Against Racism and Police Violence, and support is growing. For more information Phone 787-8442, 778-8360, 978-6636.

Please show your support for an impartial education system by filling out this form and dropping it into the suggestion box at the Royal Ontario Museum.

I agree that the ROM should not display historical events in a partial, racist, or discriminatory manner. ○

No, from what is presented in this pamphlet, I do not believe that the ROM's exhibit truly depicts African history. ○

Such an exhibit should be totally redone to represent a true and impartial view of historical events. ○

Name_____   City_____

Notes

Chapter I: Entering the Debates

1. Though it is not widely known, Cannizzo has co-curated one exhibit since *Into the Heart of Africa*. Entitled *David Livingstone and the Victorian Encounter with Africa*, the exhibit showed at the National Portrait Gallery in London in 1996. For a review see Carlisle (1996). I discuss Cannizzo's contribution in my Afterword.
2. Christie Blatchford, "Prof's Harassment Involves Us All," Toronto Sun, 19 October 1990.
3. ROM, "Letter for Publication," 1 March 1991.
4. Canadian Crossroads International (CCI) is a non-governmental, volunteer-driven, international organization working in the field of development. CCI provides cross-cultural learning experiences for volunteers from Canada and "developing" countries.
5. For overviews of these shifts in the culture of museums, see Harrison (1993) and Simpson (1996).
6. See Jones (1993) and Simpson (1996) for examples of the way in which *Into the Heart of Africa* and *The Spirit Sings* are touchstones for discussions about the politicization of museums in the West.
7. This became clear to me recently when a review of *Miscast: Negotiating Khoisan History and Material Culture*—a reflexive and controversial exhibit curated by Pippa Skotnes, which showed at the South African National Gallery in 1996— situated debates it generated about the politics of re-presenting history and negotiating post-colonial identities in relation to the *Into the Heart of Africa* controversy (Lane 1996). Moreover, reading

an analysis of responses to *Miscast* by Shannon Jackson and Steven Robins (forthcoming), I found the similarities in both the issues and our critical vocabularies for addressing them to be quite uncanny.

8. In stressing this sense of solidarity and empathy with blacks, I am not unaware of current tensions between blacks and Jews. On contemporary black-Jewish frictions see Henry Louis Gates (1993) and Cornel West (1993).

9. I would like to thank an anonymous reviewer for pointing this out to me. The fact that I had not addressed this issue is probably indicative of my own "culture of quotation marks," which takes for granted reflexive critiques of anthropology, museums, and colonialism. In this way, I am in a similar position to that of anthropologist Eva Mackey, who describes herself as an ideal viewer of *Into the Heart of Africa* (1995: 406–7).

10. Similar goals are outlined in the document "Into the Heart of Darkness: Rationale and Exhibitions Aims" (1988), which Cannizzo prepared with her curatorial team (see Crawford, Hankel and Rowse 1990: 4–5). "Into the Heart of Darkness" was the exhibit's original name, however this was changed after a marketing survey found that members of the black community considered it to be offensive.

11. On Columbus Quincentenary commemorations and counter-commemorations, see Golden (1991), Kagan (1991), and Simon (1994).

Chapter II: *Into the Heart of Africa* and the Status Quo

1. For discussions on tourism, authenticity, and appropriation, see MacCannell (1976), Stewart (1984), Handler (1986), and Neuman (1989).

2. Shops can be thought of as exhibitionary sites that appeal to a similar cultural logic. For instance, capitalizing on the appeal of an "authentic" and exotic Africa, the Canadian supermarket Loblaws sells a "President's Choice" shampoo and conditioner called "Out of Africa Botanical Secrets."

3. On the reclassification of cultural artifacts as aesthetic works of art see Ames (1986), Clifford (1988), Price (1989), Schildkrout (1989), and Kirshenblatt-Gimblett (1990). For insight into how the notion of authenticity informs Western assessments of African art, see Kasfir (1992). Responses to Sidney Kasfir by Enid Schildkrout (1992) and Johannes Fabian (1992) are germane to my interest in questioning Western constructions of, and desires for, authenticity and otherness.

4. On the need and potential for museums to become sites for addressing issues related to racism, ethnocentrism, multiculturalism, heterogeneity, and transculturation, see Cannizzo (1990a, 1991a), Gaither et al. (1989), Apter (1995), Demissie (1995), Bennett (1995), and Peirson Jones (1995).

5. This reflexive and critical approach to exhibiting culture is not appreciated by some curators. Stanley Freed, for instance, writes:

Rhetoric dominates today's deconstructionist criticism; essays reflect stimulating consciousness-raising seminars (e.g. Clifford 1989) but generally lack the nuances and respect for practical problems that come from personally creating and installing a major exhibit in a large museum. (1991: 68)

6. Simon Chung, "ROM show rejected," *Lexicon* 10 October 1990.
7. Crawford, Hankel and Rowse (1990: 32) report that the majority of visitors to *Into the Heart of Africa* were white North Americans of European descent.
8. Marjorie Halpin (1983: 265) notes that museum visitors typically spend 20–40 seconds at any one exhibit and avoid reading most labels. Visitors to *Into the Heart of Africa* typically spent about 30 minutes in the exhibit. One study found that visits ranged from 4 to 129 minutes (Crawford, Hankel and Rowse 1990: 47).
9. Schildkrout (1991) and Fulford (1991) note that the ROM is associated with "true facts." On the hegemony of objects and objectivity in museums, see Gable, Handler and Lawson (1992).
10. See Brantlinger (1985: 182) and Comaroff and Comaroff (1991: 86–99). Comaroff and Comaroff (1991) emphasize how Europeans construct negative stereotypes of Africa. In contrast, Brantlinger (1985), Miller (1985), and Torgovnick (1990) point out that positive evaluations of Africa are also made. Africa is romanticized and viewed as a site of pristine authenticity and natural innocence.
11. On intersections of humanitarian and imperial discourses see Alloula (1986), Brantlinger (1985), and Mudimbe (1989).
12. Crawford, Hankel and Rowse (1990: 48) found that 56 out of 100 visitors arrived late or left early from the slide presentation.
13. For discussions on challenges to the art/artifact dichotomy see Clifford (1988), Vogel (1988), and Price (1989).
14. The exhibit catalogue *Into the Heart of Africa* (Cannizzo 1989a) was generally well-received.
15. The *Equinox* invitation discussed above was printed on a postcard, the front of which was a cropped (head shot) version of this promotional image. Clearly, this visual image reinforced the invitation's exotic appeal. Such an advertising strategy can also be situated in the context of the gendered and sexualized nature of discourses of discovery; for instance, during the Enlightenment, exploration (like medicine), was expressed as a question of male penetration into a dark, female interior. See Philip (1991), Pratt (1992), and McClintock (1995).

Chapter III: Prelude to the Controversy

1. Negative reactions to *Into the Heart of Africa* by allies of missionaries contested Cannizzo's suggestion that missionaries were implicated in coloniz-
   ing and transforming Africa. An example of resistance to Cannizzo's
   analysis is found in an article by Doug Koop entitled "Missionaries unfairly
   maligned by ROM exhibit," and published in *Christian Week* (1991). Koop
   contests Cannizzo's use of a photograph showing missionary Mrs. Thomas
   Titcombe giving African women "a lesson how to wash clothes." Koop
   states that this photo lends itself to a "missionary-as-imperialist interpretation" (1991: 3). He questions why Cannizzo did not instead display a photograph of Mrs. Thomas Titcombe smiling and holding Nigerian twins whom
   she apparently rescued from death. Koop says that such a photo shows the
   "missionary compassion" that Cannizzo ignored. In contrast with Koop,
   I would argue that a photograph of Mrs. Titcombe holding the Nigerian twins
   is a prime example of the way in which nostalgia and sentiment can strategically be invoked to mask relations of domination (see Rosaldo 1989: 87).
2. Pauline Hill, "Out of Africa," *Key to Toronto*, November 1989. On
   December 5, 1991, long after *Into the Heart of Africa* had closed, an article
   in the *Globe and Mail* by Suanne Kelman similarly referred to the exhibit
   as the "Out of Africa show."
3. "Into the Heart of Africa," *Just Grand*, November 1989.
4. Anne Kelly, "Explore the heart of Africa in Royal Ontario Museum,"
   Sunday Democrat and Chronicle, 10 December 1989, 20; Rod Currie,
   "ROM exhibition takes exotic trip into Heart of Africa," *Kitchener-
   Waterloo Record*, 16 November 1989.
5. Paul Lovejoy, a professor of African history at York University, made a
   similar point in a letter to the ROM dated March 28, 1990. Lovejoy wrote:
   "To my mind, this exhibit is racist because it alleges to be an exhibit on
   Africa, when in fact it is an exhibit on Canadian missionaries, Canadian
   racism, and Canadian subordination to and collaboration with British
   imperialism." Some focus groups and critics also noted that the brochure
   implicitly constructed its audience as white by assuming that the colonial
   period is a "seldom remembered aspect of Canadian history." As Marlene
   Nourbese Philip points out, many African Canadians experience colonialism and its legacies in a "painfully intimate way" (1992: 105). For related
   discussions on subtle exclusions in the exhibit text and promotional materials, see Hutcheon (1994), and Mackey (1995).
6. On Rastafarian culture and themes such as diaspora identity, language, and
   resistance, see Dick Hebdige (1976, 1979). As I quote Rico in what
   follows, he makes use of the Rastafarian idiom: "I" is contextual and
   its meanings include both "me" and "you." "I and I" also has numerous
   meanings including "me," "you and me," and "we." Rico explained these

usages to me in the context of valuing equality and recognizing the presence and promise of Haile Selassie who was crowned in Ethiopia in 1930.

7. For an account of a positive experience of community consultation and
   collaboration, see Andrea Arbic (1991) on the development of the
   Africville exhibit in Nova Scotia. *Africville: A Spirit that Lives On* opened
   in October 1989 at the Art Gallery, Mount Saint Vincent University.
   It toured nationally from July 1990 to December 1992, and it is now a
   permanent display at the Black Cultural Centre in Westphal, Dartmouth.

Chapter IV: The Coalition for the Truth about Africa:
           Strategies and Challenges

1. See Sherry Ortner (1984) for an evaluation of anthropological theory
   emphasizing practice or performance. Victor Turner (1986) links the turn
   to performance with postmodern anthropology, which he describes as
   emphasizing the ethnography of speaking and social processes as opposed
   to static structures.

2. Estimates of the numbers of people who demonstrated outside the ROM
   vary greatly, depending upon the source of information. A ROM news
   release dated May 11, 1990, stated that the demonstrators numbered
   between 15 and 35 people. In contrast, the *Toronto Sun* (Tom Godfrey,
   May 6, 1990) and the *Toronto Star* (May 6, 1990) estimated the number of
   demonstrators outside of the ROM on May 5, 1990 to be about 50 people.
   The same newspapers estimated that some 75 demonstrators were present
   the following week. A member of the CFTA said to me that at peak times,
   there were some 200 demonstrators.

3. Tom Godfrey, "Cops Hurt: 2 held after ROM battle," *Toronto Sun*, 6 May
   1990, 5.: "ROM Demo Turns Ugly" was the headline on the front page of
   the same edition of the *Toronto Sun*.

4. Noel Dyck (1985b) uses the phrase "moral power" in the context of discussing fourth world performances of resistance (specifically the Saami
   Action Group in Norway). While Dyck's work (1985a, 1985b) focuses
   on symbolic resistance by indigenous peoples, his image of minorities
   turning physical powerlessness into moral power is applicable to the
   CFTA. See Henry et al. (1995) for a detailed account of (anti-black)
   racism and policing in Canada.

5. It is interesting to note that the CFTA pamphlet used quotation marks around
   words such as "savage," just as Cannizzo did in *Into the Heart of Africa* (see
   Appendix 1).

6. Journalist Christie Blatchford also referred to *Into the Heart of Africa* as
   the "Heart of Darkness exhibit" in her column in the *Toronto Sun* dated
   November 30, 1990. However, in contrast with protestors who quoted
   Conrad in the context of speaking about racism and negative portrayals

of Africa, the meaning or motivation of Blatchford's mistake is not clear to me.

7. George stocking (1974) examines references to Conrad and to *Heart of Darkness* made by Bronislaw Malinowski in his published diaries. Like Cannizzo, Stocking (1974: 284) understands *Heart of Darkness* to refer to a site of psychological crisis.

8. Crossing this divide is not always an easy task for academics, as Marie-Francoise Guédon (1983) testifies in her article entitled, "A Case of Mistaken Identity (the education of a naive museum ethnologist)."

9. The Toronto Board of Education did commend the ROM for having produced a school kit to aid teachers in preparing students to visit *Into the Heart of Africa*. The pedagogical approach of the kit is very anthropological in that it introduces themes such as: stereotyping, ethnocentrism, cultural relativism, cultural diversity, commonalities between cultures, and the historical inter-relationships between peoples.

10. See Jim Freedman (1990) for a similar evaluation of *Into the Heart of Africa*. To situate this criticism of *Into the Heart of Africa* in a larger pedagogical context see Stuart Hall (1981) and Chandra Talpade Mohanty (1989).

11. Oji Adisa, a prominent student member of the CFTA, would likely disagree with my interpretation. In a speech reported by Rebecca Spagnolo in the *Varsity* on September 24, 1990, Adisa stated: "It is possible for African people to hate white people as a result of racism, that is possible, but it is not possible for African people to be racist."

12. In *Rivers have Sources, Tress have Roots: Speaking of Racism* (1986) by Dionne Brand and Krisantha Sri Bhaggiyadatta, racism is strongly associated with looks, glances, assumptions made, and so on. See also *Black Skin White Masks* (1982) by Frantz Fanon.

13. Again, estimates of the numbers of people involved in this march vary greatly, depending upon the information source. Rashida Dhooma, writing for the *Toronto Sun* (July 15, 1990) estimated 300 people to be present. Donovan Vincent, writing for the *Toronto Star* (July 15, 1990) reported that there were about 15 Mohawks from the Six nations reserve near Brantford, and about 150 blacks.

14. Rashida Dhooma, "Anti-racism demo snarls traffic," *Toronto Sun*, 15 July 1990.: Donovan Vincent, "Natives join black protest at museum," *Toronto Star*, 15 July 1990, A8.

15. ROM, Teacher's Kit for *Into the Heart of Africa*, n.d., p.7.

Chapter V: Various Positions: Responses to the Coalition for the
                Truth about Africa

1. ROM, News Release, 11 May 1990.
2. ROM, News Release, 28 November 1990. John McNeill is presently Director of the ROM.

3. "The Pillorying of a Curator," *Globe and Mail*, 19 October 1990, A16.: Christie Blatchford, "A Surrender to Vile Harangues," *Toronto Sun*, 30 November 1990.

4. Peter Worthington, "Museum Piece," *Ottawa Sun*, 7 June 1990.: Gina Mallet, "When Culture resists the Mainstream," *Toronto Star*, 15 December 1990, G3.: Bob Phillips, "Selling our rights across the river," Ottawa Citizen, 17 December 1990.: Sid Adilman, "Bad guys discredit integrity of boards," *Toronto Star*, 24 December 1990.: Christie Blatchford, "A Surrender to Vile Harangues," *Toronto Sun*, 30 November 1990.: Christie Blatchford, "Prof's harassment involves us all," *Toronto Sun*, 19 October 1990.: "The Pillorying of a Curator," *Globe and Mail*, 19 October 1990, A16.

5. Gay Abbate, "A Commitment to Freedom of Speech and Inquiry," *University of Toronto Magazine*, Winter 1990, 30–31.

6. Peter Goddard, "The Best and Worst of 1990," *Toronto Star*, 29 December 1990, H1.: John Allemang, "The Rise of the New Puritanism," *Globe and Mail*, 2 February 1991, D1, D4.

7. Despite this depiction of Amanda Lee Brooks as a historian whose work has been suppressed, it is worth noting that Worthington quotes from an article written by Brooks that was published in *National Review*, a conservative journal edited by William F. Buckley.

8. The term "politically correct" was originally an approving phrase for the Leninist left. The term "P.C." evolved as an ironic phrase used within the left to cajole someone who strictly adhered to leftist principles and causes. The current "P.C" debates in the United States (and now in Canada) reflect a new development. For the first time, people who have no fidelity to left politics—most notably the National Association of Scholars (NAS) in the United States that claims to have 2000 members (Smith 1991:10)—employ the phrase to describe what they see as left-wing extremism on campuses. This use of the term P.C. first appeared in a small article in the *New York Times* in the fall of 1990. Months later, major American newspapers and magazines began covering the P.C. debates. A formative book in the debates is Dinesh D'Souza's *Illiberal Education: The Politics of Race and Sex on Campus* (1991). In this best-selling book, D'Souza argues that university campuses have become unbearably politicized as a new postmodern generation of professors (with roots in 1960s radicalism) have come into power. These professors and their students are characterized as having developed radical critiques of "the West" and structures of inequality, and as enforcing an atmosphere of suppression on campuses by disallowing speech and behavior that might be interpreted as racist or sexist. Speech codes, curriculum debates, and affirmative action and employment equity programs are central points of reference in the P.C. debates (see Berman 1992).

9. The fact that Fennell discusses both Cannizzo and Phillipe Rushton is significant. By analyzing Cannizzo and Rushton's predicaments as examples

of repression by politically correct students, particulars of each case are lost. I would argue for the importance of contextualizing these events. While Cannizzo is dealing critically with racist discourses, Rushton is making controversial claims about race, drawing on the authority of science. It is difficult to see how Rushton has been silenced, as Fennell claims. As a tenured academic, his academic freedom is protected. See "ROM protestors miss own point" by Donna Laframboisie in the *Toronto Star*, October 22, 1990.

10. Linda Morra, "ROM curator-prof resigns U of T post," *Varsity*, 15 October 1990.

11. The case of Harvard Professor Stephan Thernstrom is often cited. In teaching an undergraduate course called "Peopling of America," Thernstrom referred to "Indians" and "Oriental religion." Students accused Thernstrom of being racially insensitive and he then withdrew the course. *Maclean's* quotes Thernstrom as saying, "It's like being called a commie in the 1950s. Once accused, you're always suspect" (in Jenish and Lowther 1991:45). See Weiner (1991) and Beers (1991) for critical analyses of the construction of the politically correct by media and the National Association of Scholars (NAS) in the United States.

12. The following discussion is based on information drawn from minutes of the Town Meetings, a press statement that the BBPA issued August 6, 1990, and a BBPA newsletter dated June 21, 1990. Dwight Whlyie, who was Vice-President of the BBPA at the time of the ROM controversy, provided me with these materials. Members of the CFTA tended to avoid speaking to me about issues of "difference" within the black community, preferring instead to present themselves as uncontested representatives of "the black community."

13. See "The Statement of the Black Faculty Caucus" by Ted Gordon and Wahneema Lubiano (1992) for an analysis of how these issues of representation, authority, and power affect the social organization of university campuses.

14. In February 1991 there was an organizational restructuring at the ROM. Exhibit Design Services was incorporated into Exhibit and Outreach Services, and Audience Research was incorporated into the Marketing and Public Information Department.

15. "ROM apology uproar," *Toronto Sun*, 5 April 1991.

16. These interpreters in the Egypt/Nubia gallery were part of a special short-term training project funded by the Ontario government. They worked with the Education Department of the ROM during the Summer, 1992.

Afterword

1. In her contribution to the catalogue *David Livingstone and the Victorian Encounter with Africa* (1996), Cannizzo does note that Livingstone was guided by Africans to Victoria Falls. In a new development in her writing on museums, Cannizzo discusses the importance of studying processes of mutual appropriation in situations of colonial contact. In particular, Cannizzo considers ways in which Livingstone and his contemporaries may have been viewed as exotic exhibits by Africans.

2. In dealing with issues of colonialism and appropriation, curators need to be aware of the way in which museums replicate the symbolic domination of colonialism. Curators can then attempt to interrupt or reverse the colonial gaze. An unusual example of this is found in the exhibit catalogue *African Reflections: Art from Northeastern Zaire* (1990) by Enid Schildkrout and Curtis Keim. In writing about Western perceptions of the Mangbetu, Schildkrout and Keim also consider Mangbetu perceptions of Westerners. For instance, the authors note that the Mangbetu wondered about the "savagery" of German botanist George Schweinfurth (*The Heart of Africa*, 1874), as he collected African skulls to take home to European phrenologists (Schildkrout and Keim 1990: 34). See also Jane Pierson Jones' (1992, 1995) exemplary curatorial work and writing in connection with *Gallery 33: A Meeting Ground of Cultures* at the Birmingham Museum and Art Gallery. Jones makes concrete connections between theories of reflexive museology and practice.

3. See, for example, Eric Gable (1996) on Colonial Williamsburg and Thomas McEvilley (1992) on *Magiciens de la Terre*.

4. For important exceptions, see Henry et al. (1995), Mackey (1995), and Philip (1992).

5. See Mehmood (1990), MacDonald (1990), and Knowles and Van Helmond (1991) for a sense of this situation in England.

References

Abbate, Fay
1990 A Commitment to Freedom of Speech and Inquiry. *University of Toronto Magazine* Winter 30–31.

Achebe, Chinua
1977 An Image of Africa. *Massachusetts Review* 18: 94.

Aisenberg, Nadya and Mona Harrington
1988 *Women of Academe: Outsiders in the Sacred Grove.* Amherst: University of Massachusetts Press.

Alcoff, Linda
1991–2 The Problem of Speaking for Others. *Cultural Critique* (Winter): 5–32.

Alloula, Malek
1986 *The Colonial Harem.* trans. Myrna Godzich and Wlad Godzich, Minneapolis: University of Minnesota Press.

Ames, Michael
1986 *Museums, the Public and Anthropology.* New Delhi: Concept Publishing and Vancouver: University of British Columbia Press.
1991 Biculturalism in Exhibitions. *Museum Anthropology* 15(2): 7–15.
1992 *Cannibal Tours and Glass Boxes.* Vancouver: University of British Columbia Press.

Ames, Michael and Bruce Trigger
1988 Share the Blame: The Spirit Sings. Interview by Peter Gzowski. Morningside Transcript. Toronto: Canadian Broadcasting Corporation. Reprinted in *Vanguard*, April/May, 15–18.

Apter, Andrew
1995   Reading the Africa Exhibit. *American Anthropologist* 97(3): 564–66.
Arbic, Andrea
1991   Community Participation in Museums: Toward an Integrated Body of Theory and Practice. Master of Museum Studies diss., University of Toronto.
Asad, Talal.
1973   Introduction. In *Anthropology and the Colonial Encounter*, ed. Talal Asad, 10–19. Atlantic Highlands, N.J.: Humanities Press.
Asante, Molefi Kete
1987   *The Afrocentric Idea.* Philadelphia: Temple University Press.
1990   Arrogance of White Culture Ignores African Achievement. *NOW*, 19–25 July.
1992   Multiculturalism: An Exchange. In *Debating P.C.: The Controversy Over Political Correctness on College Campuses*, ed. Paul Berman, 299–314. New York: Dell Publishing.
Austin-Smith, Brenda
1990   Into the Heart of Irony. *Canadian Dimension* (October): 51–52.
Bal, Mieke
1992   Telling, Showing, Showing Off. *Critical Inquiry* Spring (18): 556–594.
Barron, Stephanie ed.
1991   *Degenerate Art: The Fate of the Avant-Garde in Nazi Germany.* Los Angeles: Los Angeles County Museum of Art.
Barthes, Roland
1988   *Mythologies.* trans. Annette Lavers, London: Paladin Books.
Bayly, Christopher
1990   Exhibiting the Imperial Image. *History Today* 40: 12–18.
Baeker, Greg, Margaret May and Mary Tivy
1992   Ontario Museums in the 1990s. *Muse* (Summer/Fall): 120–27.
Beers, David
1990   PC? B.S. Behind the Hysteria: How the Right Invented Victims of PC Police. *Mother Jones*, Sept./Oct., 34–35.
Bennett, Tony
1995   *The Birth of the Museum: History, Theory, Politics.* New York and London: Routledge.
Berman, Paul
1992   Introduction: The Debate and its Origins. In *Debating PC: The Controversy over Political Correctness on College Campuses*, ed. Paul Berman, 1–28. New York: Dell Publishing.
Bhabha, Homi
1990   The Third Space. In *Identity, Community, Culture, Difference*, ed. Jonathan Rutherford, 207–21. London: Lawrence and Wishart.

Birk, Brenda et al.
1990   Gallery Debate. Interview by Peter Gzowski. Morningside Transcript. Toronto: Canadian Broadcasting Corporation, 29 October.

Blatchford, Christie
1990   A Surrender to Vile Harangues. *Toronto Sun*, 30 November.

Bloom, Alan
1987   *The Closing of the American Mind.* New York: Simon and Schuster.

Booth, Wayne
1975   *A Rhetoric of Irony.* Chicago: University of Chicago.

Bourdieu, Pierre
1984   *Distinction: A Social Critique of the Judgement of Taste.* trans. Richard Nice, MA: Harvard University Press.

Brand, Dionne
1992   Out There. *The Malahat Review* (Fall): 115–19.

Brand, Dionne and Krisantha Sri Bhaggiyadatta
1986   *Rivers Have Sources, Trees Have Roots: Speaking of Racism.* Toronto: Cross Cultural Communication Centre.

Brantlinger, Patrick
1985   Victorians and Africans: The Genealogy of the Myth of the Dark Continent. *Critical Inquiry* 12: 166–203.
1990   *Crusoe's Footprints: Cultural Studies in Britain and America.* New York: Routledge.

Buckley, Thomas
1987   Dialogue and Shared Authority: Informants as Critics. *Central Issues in Anthropology* 7(1): 13–23.

Bunch, Lonnie
1995   Fighting the Good Fight: Museums in an Age of Uncertainty. *Museum News* March/April: 32–35, 58–62.

Butler, Shelley Ruth
1993   Contested Representations: Revisiting 'Into the Heart of Africa.' M.A. Thesis. York University.
1996   Democratizing Heritage: The South African Challenge. *Southern Africa Report* 11(3): 22–24.

Cameron, Duncan
1971   The Museum, a Temple or the Forum. *Curator* 14(1): 11–24.

Cannizzo, Jeanne
1982   Old Images/New Metaphors: The Museum in the Modern World. Ideas Transcript, Parts 1–3. Toronto: Canadian Broadcasting Corporation.
1983   The Shit Devil: Pretense and Politics Amongst West African Urban Children. In *The Celebration of Society: Perspectives on Contemporary Cultural Performance*, ed. Frank E. Manning, 125–44. Ohio: Bowling Green University Popular Press.

1987a   How Sweet It Is: Cultural Politics in Barbados. *Muse* 4(4): 22–27.
1987b   Living in the Past. Ideas Transcript. Toronto: Canadian Broad-casting Corporation.
1987c   Review of *Museums, the Public and Anthropology*, by Michael Ames. In *Muse* (Summer): 66.
1989a   *Into the Heart of Africa*. Toronto: Royal Ontario Museum.
1989b   Reading the National Collections: Museums as Cultural Texts. In *Towards the 21st Century: New Directions for Canada's National Museums*, ed. Leslie Tepper, 155–72. Ottawa: Canadian Museum of Civilization.
1990a   Into the Heart of a Controversy. *Toronto Star*, 5 June, A17.
1990b   Review of *A Museum for the Global Village*, by George F. MacDonald and R. A. J. Phillips. In *Muse* 8(3): 97.
1991a   Exhibiting Cultures: "Into the Heart of Africa." *Visual Anthropology Review* 7(1): 150–60.
1991b   To the Editor (Letter from Jeanne Cannizzo to Enid Schildkrout). *Museum Anthropology* 15(4): 5–6.
1991c   Towards an Ethnography of Museums. In *Living in a Material World*, ed. Gerald L. Pocius, 19–28. Newfoundland: Memorial University.
1996   Dr. Livingstone Collects. In *David Livingstone and the Victorian Encounter with Africa*. 139–68. London: National Portrait Gallery.

Cannon-Brookes, P.
1990   Into the Heart of Africa. *International Journal of Museum Management and Curatorship* 9(3): 292–97.

Caplan, Gerald
1991   The Sinister Crusade Against Politically Correct. *Toronto Star*, 6 June, B3.

Carlisle, Isabel
1996   Exploring the Heart of Africa. *New York Times*, July 9, x–xx.

Clifford, James
1985   Object and Selves—An Afterword. In *Objects and Others: Essays on Museums and Material Culture*, ed. George Stocking. History of Anthropology, no. 3, 586–95. Madison: University of Wisconsin Press.
1986   Partial Truths. In *Writing Culture: The Poetics and Politics of Ethnography*, eds. James Clifford and George Marcus, 1–26. California: University of California Press.
1987   Of Other Peoples: Beyond the Salvage Paradigm. In *The Anti-Aesthetic: Essays on Postmodern Culture*, ed. Hal Foster, 121–30. Washington: Bay Press.
1988   *The Predicament of Culture: Twentieth-Century Ethnography, Literature, and Art*. MA: Harvard University Press.

1991   Four Northwest Coast Museums: Travel Reflections. In *Exhibiting Cultures: The Poetics and Politics of Museum Display*, eds. Ivan Karp and Steven Lavine, 212–54. Washington: Smithsonian stitution Press.

1992   Travelling Cultures. In *Cultural Studies*, eds. Lawrence Grossberg, Cary Nelson and Paula Treicher, 96–112. New York: Routledge.

1997   *Routes: Travel and Translation in the Late Twentieth Century.* Cambridge MA: Harvard University Press.

Comaroff, Jean and John Comaroff

1991   *Of Revelation and Revolution: Christianity, Colonialism, and Consciousness in South Africa.* Vol. 1. Chicago: The University of Chicago Press.

Conrad, Joseph

1988   *Heart of Darkness.* Robert Kimbrough, ed. Norton Critical edition. New York: Norton.

Cooper, Afua

1992   *Memories Have Tongue.* Toronto: Sister Vision Press.

Crapanzano, Vincent

1985   *Waiting: The Whites of South Africa.* New York: Vintage Books.

Crawford, Belinda, Lillian Hankel and Gloria Rowse

1990   *Into the Heart of Africa*: An Evaluation. Royal Ontario Museum: Exhibits Division.

Crean, Susan

1991   Taking the Missionary Position. *Fuse* 24(6): 23–8.

Cruikshank, Julie

1992   Oral Tradition and Material Culture. *Anthropology Today* 8(3): 5–9.

Cruise, James E.

1977   Even ROM Wasn't Built in a Day: Retrospect and Prospect at the Royal Ontario Museum on the Eve of Expansion. *Rotunda* 10(2): 4–11.

Da Breo, Hazel

1989/90a   Hazel A. Da Breo Interviews Dr. Jeanne Cannizzo. *Fuse* Winter, 36–37.

1989/90b   Royal Spoils: The Museum Confronts its Colonial Past. *Fuse* Winter, 28–36.

1990   Review of *Into the Heart of Africa*, In *Culture* X(1): 104–5.

de Certeau, Michel

1988   *The Practice of Everyday Life.* trans. by Steven Rendall. Berkeley: University of California Press.

Demissie, Fassil

1995   An Enchanting Darkness: A New Representation of Africa. *American Anthropologist* 97(3): 559–64.

De Witt, Karen
  1995a   Library Gives in to Protests and Closes Slavery Exhibition. *New York Times*, 21 December, A16.
  1995b   Smithsonian Scales Back Exhibit of Plane in Atomic Bomb Attack. *New York Times*, 31 January, A1, C19.
Dickerson, Amima
  1991   Redressing the Balance. *Museums* (February): 21–23.
Dinesen, Isak
  1985   *Out of Africa*. New York: Vintage.
Diop, Cheikh Anta
  1974   *The African Origin of Civilization*. trans. Mercer Cook, New York: Lawrence and Hill & Co.
Dominguez, Virginia
  1987   Of Other Peoples: Beyond the Salvage Paradigm. In *Discussions in Contemporary Culture* Vol. 1, ed. Hal Foster, 131–37. Seattle: Bay Press.
Douglas, Mary
  1970   *Purity and Danger: An Analysis of Concepts of Pollution and Taboo*. Harmondworth: Penguin.
Doxtator, Deborah
  1993   The Rebirth of a Native Exhibit Inside a White Institution: Fluffs and Feathers Goes to the ROM. Paper presented at the Canadian Anthropology Society Annual Conference. Toronto, 8 May.
D'Souza, Dinesh
  1991   *Illiberal Education: The Politics of Race and Sex on Campus*. New York: Free Press.
Dyck, Noel
  1985a   Aboriginal Peoples and Nation-States: An Introduction to the Analytical Issues. In *Indigenous Peoples and the Nation State: Fourth World Politics in Canada, Australia and Norway*, ed. Noel Dyck, 1–26. St. John's, Newfoundland: Institute of Social and Economic Research, Memoral University.
  1985b   Ethnodrama and the 'Fourth World': The Saami Action Group in Norway, 1979–1981. In *Indigenous Peoples and the Nation State: Fourth World Politics in Canada, Australia and Norway*, ed. Noel Dyck, 190–235. St. John's, Newfoundland: Institute of Social and Economic Research, Memoral University.
Eagleton, Terry
  1983   *Literary Theory: An Introduction*. England: Basil Blackwell.
Early, Gerald
  1992   Their Malcolm, My Problem: On the Abuses of Afrocentrism and Black Anger. *Harper's Magazine*, December, 62–73.

Edinborough, Arnold
1989   Exhibition on Heart of Africa a ROM Triumph. *Anglican Journal* (December): 19.
Evans, Kristi S.
1992   The Argument of Images: Historical Representation in Solidarity Underground Postage, 1981–87. *American Ethnologist* 19(4): 749–67.
Fabian, Johannes
1983   *Time and the Other: How Anthropology Makes Its Object.* New York: Columbia University Press.
1992   Quibbles and Questions. Response to Kasfir. *African Arts* 25(3): 22–24.
Fanon, Frantz
1982   *Black Skin, White Masks.* Evergreen Edition. trans. Charles Lam Markmann. New York: Grove Press.
Faris, James C.
1988   ART/Artifact: On the Museum and Anthropology. *Current Anthropology* 29(5): 775–79.
Fennell, Tom
1991   The Silencers. *Maclean's*, 27 May, 40–43.
Fiske, John
1989   *Understanding Popular Culture.* London: Routledge.
Foster, Hal, ed.
1983   *The Anti-Aesthetic: Essays on Postmodern Culture.* Washington: Bay Press.
Freed, Stanley
1991   Everyone is Breathing on our Vitrines: Problems and Prospects of Museum Anthropology. *Curator* 34(1): 58–80.
Freedman, Adele
1989   A Revealing Journey Through Time and Space. *Globe and Mail*, 17 November, C1.
Freedman, Jim
1990   Bringing it all Back Home: A Commentary on *Into the Heart of Africa. Museum Quarterly* 18(1): 39–43.
Fulford, Robert
1991   Into the Heart of the Matter. *Rotunda* (Summer): 19–28.
Gable, Eric
1996   Maintaining boundaries, or 'mainstreaming' black history in a white museum. In *Theorizing Museums: Representing identity and diversity in a changing world*, eds. S. MacDonald and G. Fyfe, 177–202. Oxford: Blackwell/The Sociological Review.

Gable, Eric, Richard Handler, and Anna Lawson
1992   On the Uses of Relativism: Fact, Conjecture, and the Black and White Histories at Colonial Williamsburg. *American Ethnologist* 19(4): 791–805.
Gaither, Barry et al.
1989   Voicing Varied Opinions: Four Museum Professionals Probe Some of the Difficult Issues Related to Cultural Diversity. Round Table Discussion. *Museum News* (March/April): 49–52.
Garfield, Donald
1989   Dimensions of Diversity. *Museum News* (March/April): 43–48.
Gates, Henry Louis
1991   Canon Formation and the Afro-American Tradition. In *The Bounds of Race: Perspectives on Hegemony and Resistance.* ed. Dominick LaCapra, 17–38. Ithaca: Cornell University Press.
1992a   Pluralism and its Discontents. *Profession* (MLA): 35–38.
1992b   Whose Canon Is It, Anyway? In *Debating P.C.: The Controversy Over Political Correctness on College Campuses*, ed. Paul Berman, 190–200. New York: Dell Publishing.
1993   Black Intellectuals, Jewish Tensions: A Weaving of Identities. *New York Times*, 14 April, A15.
Gilroy, Paul
1987   *'There Ain't No Black in the Union Jack': The Cultural Politics of Race and Nation.* London: Hutchinson.
Ginsburg, Faye
1989   *Contested Lives: the Abortion Debate in an American Community.* Berkeley: University of California Press.
Giroux, Henry
1988   Postmodernism and the Discourse of Educational Criticism. *Journal of Education* 170(3): 5–29.
1992   Post-Colonial Ruptures and Democratic Possibilities: Multi culturalism as Anti-Racist Pedagogy. *Cultural Critique* (Spring): 5–39.
Goldberg, Paul
1996   Historical Shows on Trial; Who Judges? *New York Times*, 11 February.
Golden, Tim
1991   Columbus Landed, er, Looted, uh—Rewrite! *New York Times*, 6 October, 1 and 36.
Gordon, Ted and Wahneema Lubiano
1992   The Statement of the Black Faculty Caucus. In *Debating P.C.: The Controversy Over Political Correctness on College Campuses*, ed. Paul Berman, 249–57. New York: Dell Publishing.
Graff, Gerald
1992   *Beyond the Culture Wars: How Teaching the Conflicts Can Revitalize American Education.* New York: W. W. Norton.

Grant, Laurence
  1990   Review of *Into the Heart of Africa. Muse* (Summer): 78–80.
Guedon, Marie-Francoise
  1983   A Case of Mistaken Identity (the Education of a Naive Museum
         Ethnologist). In *Consciousness and Inquiry: Ethnology and
         Canadian Realities.* ed. Frank Manning, 253–61. Ottawa: National
         Museum of Canada.
Gurian, Elaine Heumann
  1990   Noodling Around with Exhibition Opportunities. In *Exhibiting
         Cultures: The Poetics and Politics of Museum Display*, eds. Ivan
         Karp and Steven Lavine, 176–90. Washington: Smithsonian
         Institution Press.
Hall, Stuart
  1981   Teaching Race. In *The School in the Multiracial Society: A Reader*,
         eds. Alan James and Robert Joffcoate, 58–69. New York: Harper
         and Row in assoc. With The Open University Press.
  1992   Cultural Identity and Diaspora. In *Identity, Community, Culture,
         Difference,* Jonathan Rutherford, 222–37. London: Lawrence and
         Wishart.
Halpin, Marjorie
  1983   Anthropology as Artifact. In *Consciousness and Inquiry: Ethnology
         and Canadian Realities.* ed. Frank Manning, 262–75. Ottawa:
         National Museum of Canada.
  n.d.   *Fragments: Reflections on Collecting.* UBC Museum of
         Anthropology, Museum Note No. 31.
Handler, Richard
  1986   Authenticity. *Anthropology Today* 2(1): 2–4.
  1988   Review of Museums, the Public and Anthropology, by Michael
         Ames. In *American Anthropologist* 90(4): 1035–36.
Harris, Eddy L.
  1992   *Native Stranger: A Black American's Journey Into the Heart of
         Africa.* New York: Simon and Schuster.
Harris, Neil
  1996   Dreaming By Committee. *Museum News* March/April: 66–70.
Harris, Olivia and Peter Gow
  1985   The British Museum's Representation of Amazonian Indians.
         Anthropology Today 1(5): 1–2.
Harrison, Faye V.
  1991   Anthropology as an Agent of Transformation: Introductory
         Comments and Queries. In *Decolonizing Anthropology: Moving
         further toward an Anthropology for Liberation*, ed. Faye Harrison,
         1–13. Washington D.C.: Association of Black Anthropologists,
         AAA.

Harrison, Julia
   1993   Ideas of Museums in the 1990s. *Museum Management and Curatorship* 13: 160–76.

Harrison, Julia et al.
   1988   The Spirit Sings and the Future of Anthropology. *Anthropology Today* 4(6): 6–9.

Harvey, Kerridwen
   1989   New York Shows the Primitive: The Contextualist/Formalist Debate in Recent Exhibitions. Unpublished manuscript.

Hebdige, Dick
   1976   Reggae, Rastas & Rudies. In *Resistance Through Rituals: Youth Sub-cultures in Post-War Britain*, eds. S. Hall and T. Jefferson, 135–53. New York: Holmes and Mies.

   1979   *Subculture: The Meaning of Style*. London: Methuen and Co.

Henry, Frances et al.
   1995   *The Colour of Democracy: Racism in Canadian Society*. Canada: Harcourt Brace.

Hitt, Jack et al.
   1989   Who Needs the Great Works? *Harper's Magazine* (Forum), September, 44–52.

hooks, bell
   1990   *Yearning: Race, Gender, and Cultural Politics*. Boston MA: South End Press.

Hrdy, Sarah Blaffer
   1992   The Myth of Mother Love. Review of *Death Without Weeping: The Violence of Everyday Life in Brazil*, by Nancy Scheper-Hughes. In *New York Times Book Review*, 30 August, 11.

Hume, Christopher
   1989   ROM looks into Heart of Africa. *Toronto Star*, 17 November, E3 and E22.

   1990   Rejection of ROM Show not a Defeat for Racism. *Toronto Star*, 29 September, F3.

Hutcheon, Linda
   1989   *The Politics of Postmodernism*. London: Routledge.

   1991   *Splitting Images: Contemporary Canadian Ironies*. Oxford: Oxford University Press.

   1994   The Post Always Rings Twice: The Postmodern and the Post-colonial. *Textual Practice* 8(2): 205–38.

   1995   *Irony's Edge: The Theory and Politics of Irony*. London: Routledge.

Inglis, Stephan
   1990   Editorial Note. *Culture* 10(1): 103.

Jackson, Shannon and Steven Robins
  forthcoming Miscast: The Place of the Museum in Negotiating the "Bushman" Past and Present. *Critical Arts.*
Jenkinson, Peter
  1989 Material Culture, People's History and Populism. In *Museum Studies in Material Culture*, ed. Susan Pearce, 139–52. London: Leicester University Press.
Jones, Anna Laura
  1993 Exploding Canons: The Anthropology of Museums. *Annual Review of Anthropology* 22: 201–20.
Jones, Jane Pierson
  1992 The Colonial Legacy and the Community: The Gallery 33 Project. In *Museums and Communities: The Politics of Public Culture*, eds Ivan Karp, Christine Mullen Kreamer, Steven D. Lavine, 221–41. Washington: Smithsonian Institution Press.
  1995 Communicating and Learning in Galley 33: Evidence From a Visitor Study. In *Museum, Media, Message*, ed. Eileen Hooper-Greenhill, 260–74. New York: Routledge.
Jones, Jane Pierson and Anandi Ramamurthy
  1992 Multiculturalism Incarnate. *Museums Journal* (1): 33.
Jordanova, Ludmilla
  1989 Objects of Knowledge: A Historical Perspective on Museums. In *The New Museology*, ed. Peter Vergo, 22–40. London: Reaktion Books.
Kagan, Richard L.
  1991 The Discovery of Columbus. *New York Times Book Review*, 6 October, 3 and 27–29.
Karp, Ivan
  1990 Culture and Representation. In *Exhibiting Cultures: The Poetics and Politics of Museum Display*, eds. Ivan Karp and Steven D. Lavine, 11–24. Washington: Smithsonian Institution Press.
  1990 Other Cultures in Museum Perspective. In *Exhibiting Cultures: The Poetics and Politics of Museum Display*, eds. Ivan Karp and Steven D. Lavine, 373–85. Washington: Smithsonian Institution Press.
  1992 Introduction: Museums and Communities: The Politics of Public Culture. In *Museums and Communities: The Politics of Public Culture*, eds. Ivan Karp, Christine Mullen Kreamer, Steven D. Lavine, 1–18. Washington: Smithsonian Institution Press.
Kasfir, Sidney
  1992 African Art and Authenticity: A Text with a Shadow. *African Arts* 25(2): 41–53.

Keefer, Michael H.
1992   Ellis on Deconstruction: A Second Opinion. *English Studies in Canada* (Reader's Forum) 18(1): 83–103.

Kimmelman, Michael
1991   Old West, New Twist At the Smithsonian. *New York Times*, 26 May, II 1, 27.

Kincaid, Jamaica
1991   Foreword to *Babouk*, by Guy Endore. New York: Monthly Review Press.

Kirshenblatt-Gimblett, Barbara
1990a   Afterword: Other Places, Other Times. In *City Play*, Amanda Dargan and Steven Zeitlin, 175–206. New Brunswick and London: Rutgers Press.
1990b   Objects of Ethnography. In *Exhibiting Cultures: The Poetics and Politics of Museum Display*, eds. Ivan Karp and Steven Lavine, 386–443. Washington: Smithsonian Institution Press.

Knowles, Loraine and Marij van Hehmond
1991   Staying Power. *Museums* (April): 16–17.

Kondo, Dorinne K.
1990   *Crafting Selves: Power, Gender, and Discourses on Identity in a Japanese Workplace.* Chicago: The University of Chicago Press.

Koop, Doug
1991   Missionaries Unfairly Maligned by ROM Exhibit. *Christian Week*, 8 January, 3.

Kreps, Christina
1988   Decolonizing Anthropology Museums: The Tropenmuseum, Amsterdam. *Museum Studies Journal* 3(2): 56–62.

LaCapra, Dominick
1989   *Soundings in Critical Theory.* Ithaca and London: Cornell University Press.
1991   Introduction. In *The Bounds of Race: Perspectives on Hegemony and Resistance* ed. Dominick LaCapra. Ithaca: Cornell University Press.

Lalla, Hari and John Myers
1990   Report on Royal Ontario Museum's Exhibit "Into the Heart of Africa." Toronto Board of Education, May.

Lambek, Michael
1990   Letter for publication to Paul Thompson, Principal of Scarborough College. University of Toronto, 7 October.

Lane, Paul
1996   Breaking the Mould? Exhibiting Khoisan in Southern African museums. *Anthropology Today* 12(5): 3–10.

Lavine, Stevine D.
1989   Museums and Multiculturalism: Who Is in Control? *Museum News* March/April: 37–42.

Levin, Kim
  1989 Bring 'Em Back Alive. In *Art/Artifact: African Art in Anthropological Collections*, ed. Susan Vogel, 204–5. New York: Abrams/Center for African Art.

Levin, Michael
  1990 Irony (and, of, in) Artifacts. Review of Into the Heart of Africa. *Culture* 10(1): 103–4.

Little, Kenneth
  1991 On Safari: The Visual Politics of a Tourist Representation. In *The Varieties of Sensory Experience: A Sourcebook in the Anthropology of the Senses*, ed. David Howes, 149–63. Toronto, University of Toronto Press.
  1995 Talking Circus not Culture: The Politics of Identity in European Circus Discourse. *Qualitative Inquiry* 1(3): 346–59.

Loughery, John
  1992 The Fate of the Avant-Garde. *The Hudson Review* (Winter): 623–30.

Lowenthal, David
  1985 *The Past is a Foreign Country.* New York: Cambridge University Press.

Lucs, Sandra
  1990 Another look at ... Into the Heart of Africa. *Museum Quarterly* (August): 35–39.

Lyons, Harriet and Andrew Lyons
  n.d. Postmodern Anthropology: The Road to Hell and the Crisis at the ROM. Unpublished manuscript.

MacCannell, Dean
  1976 *The Tourist: A New Theory of the Leisure Class.* New York: Schocken Books.

MacDonald, Sally
  1990 Telling White Lies. *Museums Journal* 90(9): 34–35.

Mack, John
  1990 *Emil Torday and the Art of the Congo 1900–1909.* London: British Museum.

Mackey, Eva
  1995 Postmodernism and Cultural Politics in a Multicultural Nation: Contests over Truth in the *Into the Heart of Africa* Controversy. *Public Culture* 7: 403–31.

Manning, Frank
  1989a Carnival in the City: The Caribbeanization of Urban Landscapes. *Urban Resources* 5(3): 3–8 and 43.
  1989b Spectacle. In *International Encyclopedia of Communications.* Oxford: Oxford University Press. (4): 137–44.
  1986 *Anthropology as Cultural Critique: An Experimental Moment in the Human Sciences.* Chicago: The University of Chicago.

Marcus, George and Michael Fischer
    1986 *Anthropology as Cultural Critique: An Experimental Moment in the Human Sciences.* Chicago: The University of Chicago Press.
McClelland, Janet
    1990 Uncovering a Hidden Curriculum? *Role Call*, April, 10.
McClintock, Anne
    1995 *Imperial Leather: Race, Gender and Sexuality in the Colonial Context.* New York: Routledge.
McEvilley, Thomas
    1989 ART/Artifact: What Makes Something Art? *In Art/Artifact: African Art in Anthropological Collections*, ed. Susan Vogel, 200–3. New York: Abrams/Center for African Art.
    1992 *Art and Otherness: Crisis in Cultural Identity.* New York: Documentext, McPherson and Company.
Mehmood, Tariq
    1990 Trophies of Plunder. *Museums Journal* 90(9): 27–29.
Miller, Christopher
    1989 *Blank Darkness.* Chicago: University of Chicago Press.
Minh-ha Trinh T.
    1987 Of Other Peoples: Beyond the Salvage Paradigm. *In Discussions in Contemporary Culture.* Vol. 1, ed. Hal Foster, 138–41. Seattle: Bay Press.
Mitchell, Nancy Marie
    1990 Oppositional Theory and Minority Museums. Unpublished manuscript.
Mitchell, Timothy
    1988 *Colonising Egypt.* Cambridge: Cambridge University Press.
    1989 The World as Exhibition. *Society for Comparative Study of Society and History* 31(2): 217–36.
Mohanty, Chandra Talpade
    1989/90 On Race and Voice: Challenges for Liberal Education in the 1990s. *Cultural Critique* (Winter): 179–208.
Mohanty, S.P.
    1989 Us and Them: On the Philosophical Bases of Political Criticism. *Yale Journal of Criticism* 2(2): 1–31.
Mudimbe, Valentine
    1988 *The Invention of Africa: Gnosis, Philosophy and the Order of Knowledge.* Bloomington, Indiana: Indiana University Press.
Muecke, Douglas Colin
    1970 *Irony.* London: Methuen.
Munjeri, Dawson
    1990 Refocusing or Reorientation? The Exhibit or the Populace: Zimbabwe on the Threshold. In *Exhibiting Cultures: The Poetics*

and Politics of Museum Display, eds. Ivan Karp and Steven Lavine, 444–56. Washington: Smithsonian Institution Press.

Myerhoff, Barbara
  1986   "Life Not Death in Venice": Its Second Life. In *The Anthropology of Experience*, eds. Victor Turner and Edward M. Bruner, 261–66. Chicago: University of Illinois Press.
  1987   Surviving Stories: Reflections on Number Our Days. *Tikkun* 2(5): 19–25.

Nazareth, Errol
  1990   Royal Ontario Museum: Showcase Showdown. *NOW*, 29 March– 4 April, 10–12.

Nelson, Cary, Paula A. Treichler and Lawrence Grossberg
  1992   Cultural Studies: An Introduction. In *Cultural Studies*. eds. Lawrence Grossberg, Cary Nelson and Paula Treichler, 1–22. New York: Routledge.

Neumann, Mark
  1988   Wandering Through the Museum: Experience and Identity in a Spectator Culture. *Borderlines* 12: 19–27.

Nicks, Trudy
  1992   Partnerships in Developing Cultural Resources: Lessons from the Task Force on Museums and First Peoples. *Culture* XII(1): 87–94.

Nosov, Susan
  1992   Educating for Change: Jewish Women Confronting Racism. *Fireweed* 106–9.

Nunley, John
  1991   Review of *Into the Heart of Africa* (catalogue). *African Arts* XXIV(1): 35–36 and 90–91.

O'Connell, Mary
  1991   Politically Correct. Transcript Sunday Morning Program. Toronto: Canadian Broadcasting Corporation.

Ogg, Anthony
  1987   Slaughtering the Golden Calves. *Journal of Education in Museums* 7: 16–19.

O'Rourke, Dennis
  1987   *Cannibal Tours*. Los Angeles: Direct Cinema.

Ortner, Sherry B.
  1984   Theory in Anthropology since the Sixties. *Society for Comparative Study of Society and History* 126–66.

Ortiz, Alfonzo
  1991   American Indians and the Columbian Quincentenary Exhibit. Paper presented as part of the symposium "The Columbian Quincentenary in Comparative Perspective" at the Annual Meeting of the American Anthropological Assocation, Chicago: 20–24 November.

Ottenberg, Simon
    1991   Review of *Into the Heart of Africa. African Arts* XXIV(3): 79–82.
Palmer, Richard
    1977   Toward a Postmodern Hermeneutics of Performance. In *Performance in Postmodern Culture*, eds. Michel Benamou and Charles Caramello, 19–32. Wisconsin: Coda Press.
Payne, Robert
    1990   Exhibit calls for balance. *Toronto Sun*, 22 July.
Philip, Marlene Nourbese
    1990   *Looking for Livingstone: An Odyssey of Silence.* Toronto: The Mercury Press.
    1991   Museum could have avoided culture clash. *Toronto Star*, 14 January, A13.
    1992   *Frontiers: Essays and Writings on Racism and Culture.* Stratford: Mercury Press.
Pollitt, Kathy
    1992   Why Do We Read? In *Debating P.C.: The Controversy Over Political Correctness on College Campuses*, ed. Paul Berman, 201–14. New York: Dell Publishing.
Pratt, Mary Louise
    1993   *Imperial Eyes: Travel Writing and Transculturation.* London: Routledge.
Price, Sally
    1989   *Primitive Art in Civilized Places.* Chicago: University of Chicago Press.
Ravitch, Diane
    1992   Multiculturalism: E Pluribus Plures. In *Debating P.C.: The Controversy Over Political Correctness on College Campuses*, ed. Paul Berman, 271–98. New York: Dell Publishing.
Rickards, Colin
    1989a Into the Heart of Africa. *Share*, 8 November.
    1989b Africa—through Canadian eyes. *Share*, 29 November.
Roach, Charles
    1990   Into the heart of the controversy. *Toronto Star*, 5 June, A17.
Rodman, Margaret Critchlow
    1993   A Critique of "Place" through Field Museum's Pacific Exhibits. *The Contemporary Pacific* 5(2): 243–74.
Rorty, Richard
    1989   *Contingency, irony, and solidarity.* Cambridge: Cambridge University Press.
Rosaldo, Renato
    1989   *Culture and Truth: The Remaking of Social Analysis.* Boston MA: Beacon Press.

Rothschild, Joyce and J. Allen Whitt
   1986   *The Cooperative Workplace: Potentials and Dilemmas of Organizational Democracy and Participation.* Cambridge: Cambridge University Press.
Ruffins, Fath Davis
   1997   Culture Wars Won and Lost: Ethnic Museums on the Mall, Part 1: The National Holocaust Museum and the National Museum of the American Indian. *Radical History Review* 68: 79–100.
Said, Edward
   1989   Representing the Colonilzed: Anthropology's Interlocutors. *Critical Inquiry* 15: 205–23.
   1992   The Politics of Knowledge. In *Debating P.C.: The Controversy Over Political Correctness on College Campuses*, ed. Paul Berman, 172–89. New York: Dell Publishing.
   1993a *Culture and Imperialism.* New York: Knopf.
   1993b Imperialism and After: Europe, the U.S. and the Rest of Us. Paper presented at York University, Ontario, 10 February.
Samarin, William
   1990   African exhibit indicts Canadian missionaries for arrogance. *Christian Week*, 12 June, 14.
Scarlett, Vivian
   1990   Invitation Refused. (Letter) *Share*, 13 June.
Schildkrout, Enid
   1989   Art as Evidence: A Brief History of the American Museum of Natural History African Collection. In *Art/Artifact: African Art in Anthropological Collections*, ed. Susan Vogel, 153–60. New York: Abrams/Center for African Art.
   1991a Ambiguous Messages and Ironic Twists: Into the Heart of Africa and The Other Museum. *Museum Anthropology* 15(2): 16–23.
   1991b Reply from Enid Schildkrout. *Museum Anthropology* (15) 4: 6.
   1992a A Curator Talks Back. Response to Kasfir. *African Arts* 25(3):14–18.
   1992b Revisiting Emil Torday's Congo: "Images of Africa" at the British Museum. *African Arts* 25(1): 60–69, 99.
Schildkrout, Enid and Curtis A. Keim
   1990   *African Reflections: Art from Northeastern Zaire.* Seattle: University of Washington Press and the American Museum of Natural History.
Scholte, Bob
   1972   Toward a Reflexive and Critical Anthropology. In *Reinventing Anthropology*, ed. Del Hymes, 430–57. New York: Pantheon Books.

Skotnes, Pippa ed.
  1996   *Miscast: Negotiating the Presence of the Bushmen.* Cape Town:
         University of Cape Town Press.
Scott, James
  1986   Everyday Forms of Peasant Resistance. *Journal of Peasant
         Studies*, 14(2): 5–35.
Scott, Joan Wallach
  1991   The Campaign Against Political Correctness: What's Really at
         Stake? *Change* (November/December): 30–43.
Shelton, Anthony
  1990   In the Lair of the Monkey: Notes Towards a Postmodern
         Museography. In *Objects of Knowledge* ed. Susan Pearce, 78–102.
         London: Athlone Press.
Simon, Roger I
  1994   Forms of Insurgence in the Production of Popular Memories:
         The Columbus Quincentenary and the Pedagogy of Counter-
         Commemoration. In *Between Borders: Pedagogy and the Politics
         of Cultural Studies*, eds. Henry Giroux and Peter McLaren,
         127–42. New York and London: Routledge.
Simpson, Moira
  1996   *Making Representations: Museums in the Post-Colonial Era.*
         London: Routledge.
Smith, Doug
  1991   The New McCarthyism. *Canadian Dimension* (September): 8–13.
Sontag, Susan
  1977   *On Photography.* New York: Anchor Books, Doubleday.
Spivak, Gayatri
  1990   *The Post-Colonial Critic: Interviews, Strategies, Dialogues.* Sarah
         Harasym, ed. New York: Routledge.
Stewart, Susan
  1984   *On Longing: Narratives of the miniature, the gigantic, the sou-
         venir, the collection.* Baltimore: John Hopkins University Press.
Stocking, George W.
  1974   "Empathy and Antipathy in the Heart of Darkness" In *Readings in
         the History of Anthropology*, ed. Regna Darnell, 281–87. New
         York: Harper and Row.
  1985   *Objects and Others: Essays on Museums and Material Culture.*
         History of Anthropology, no. 3. Madison: University of Wisconsin
         Press.
Tawadros, Giliane
  1990   Is the Past a Foreign Country? *Museums Journal* 90(9): 30–31.

Taylor, John
   1991   Don't Blame Me! The New Culture of Victimization. *New York*,
          3 June, 26–34.
Torgovnick, Marianna
   1990   *Gone Primitive: Savage Intellects, Modern Lives.* Chicago: The
          University of Chicago Press.
Turner, Victor
   1977   Frame, Flow and Reflection: Ritual and Drama as Public
          Liminality. In *Performance in Postmodern Culture*, eds. Michel
          Benamou and Charles Caramello, 33–58. Wisconsin: Coda Press.
   1986   *The Anthropology of Performance.* New York: PAJ Publications.
Urry, John
   1990   *The Tourist Gaze: Leisure and Travel in Contemporary Societies.*
          London: Sage Publications.
Vellela, Tony
   1988   *New Voices: Student Political Activism in the 80s and 90s.* Boston
          MA: South End Press.
Vogel, Susan
   1989a African Art: Western Eyes. In *Art/Artifact: African Art in
          Anthropological Collections*, ed. Susan Vogel, 198–99. New
          York: Abrams/Center for African Art.
   1989b Introduction. In *Art/Artifact: African Art in Anthropological
          Collections*, ed. Susan Vogel, 11–17. New York: Abrams/Center
          for African Art.
   1990   Always True to the Object, in Our Fashion. In *Exhibiting Cultures:
          The Poetics and Politics of Museum Display*, eds. Ivan Karp and
          Steven Lavine, 191–204. Washington: Smithsonian Institution Press.
Weil, Stephen E.
   1990   *Rethinking the Museum.* Washington and London: Smithsonian
          Institution.
Weiner, Jon
   1991   What Happened at Harvard. *The Nation*, 30 Sept., 384–88.
West, Cornel
   1992   Diverse New World. In *Debating P.C.: The Controversy Over
          Political Correctness on College Campuses*, ed. Paul Berman,
          326–32. New York: Dell Publishing.
   1993   Black Intellectuals, Jewish Tensions: How to End the Impasse.
          New York Times, 14 April, A15.
Wiginton, Colin
   1991   Art is not Enough: Museums in the Age of AIDS. Master of
          Museum Studies diss., University of Toronto.

Wilford, John Noble
    1992   Nubian Treasures Reflect Black Influence on Egypt. *New York Times*, 11 February, B5 and B8.
Williams, Raymond
    1983   *Keywords: A Vocabulary of Culture and Society.* London: Fontana Press.
Worthington, Peter
    1990   Museum Piece. *Ottawa Sun*, 7 June.
Young, Cuyler T.
    1993   *Into the Heart of Africa*: The Director's Perspective. *Curator* 36(3): 174–88.

Index

Achebe, Chinua, 69
African and Caribbean Student
    Association, 91
African Reflections, 87, 115
Africville, 111
Afrocentrism, 68, 71–3
Aisenberg, Nadya and Mona Harrington,
    17, 83
Albequerque Museum of Natural
    History, 2, 81
Alloula, Malek, 38
Alonzo, Hanzel, 76
Akwesasne Warrior Society, 77
Ames, Michael, 16, 33
Anglican Journal, 42
Anthropology, 7–10, 16, 17, 40, 57–9,
    67, 711, 81–2, 100, 111, 112
Arbic, Andrea, 49, 111
Art/Artifact, 27
Asante, Molefi Kete, 68, 72
Authenticity, 15–16, 31, 34, 48, 50, 108

Banfield, Reverend, 23, 38, 43
Bayly, Christopher, 37
Beresford, Lord, 25, 26, 41, 65, 80
Bhabha, Homi, 45, 46, 78

Birmingham Museum and Art Gallery,
    31
Black, Ayanna, 50
Black Action Defense Committee, 76, 89
Black Business and Professional
    Association, 88–91, 94
Black Secretariat, 49
Blatchford, Christie, 84, 111, 113
Bloom, Allan, 82
Blyden, Edward, 74–5
Bourdieu, Pierre, 20
Brand, Dionne, 77, 112
British Columbia Museums Association,
    17
Buckley, William F., 113
Bush, George, 86

Cameron, Duncan, 1–2, 12
Canadian African Newcomer
    Association, 49
Canadian Crossroads International, 5
Canadian Museum of Civilization, 2, 81
Cannizzo, Jeanne, 2–4, 6, 7, 9, 10, 16–20,
    23, 25, 27–8, 31–5, 37–40, 41, 42–3,
    44, 45, 50, 62, 64, 65, 67, 75, 81–3,
    85, 86, 87, 88, 92, 93, 94, 97, 98,
    107, 108, 109, 110, 115